Table of Contents

Gifts of the Holy Spirit

With Rick E Leis

Introducing the author:

Rick has been in ministry for over 30 years in both Pentecostal and Charismatic churches. As a Missouri Synod Lutheran he graduated from the Concordia pre-seminary program at Valparaiso University in Indiana and has done graduate work at Concordia Lutheran Seminary and at Oral Roberts seminary. He now resides in Tucson, Arizona with his wife Marilyn of 42 years. Rick and Marilyn have together six children; the last three were adopted from China. Rick and Marilyn were blessed to have traveled to China on three different occasions. In 1991 Rick started a pastor's prayer organization; it grew very rapidly and spread into other countries as well. Coalition of Prayer Network International was instrumental in bringing reconciliation between the San Carlos Apache and representative people who slaughtered helpless people. Among the Apache unreconciled offense is considered to be active until reconciliation takes Place. It is as if the massacre happened yesterday.[1] Rick is well known in Charismatic and Mainline churches for his teaching on intercessory prayer and related

---

[1] Camp Grant Massacre or the San Creek Massacre – Reconciliation took almost four years and involved the White Mountain Apache, San Carlos Apache, Hopi, Navaho and Desert Kawia

experiences. He has presided over several pastoral organizations. Among them was the Tucson Association of Evangelicals for four terms and President of Southwest Ministers Conference. Between the two, there were over 600 churches. Rick continues to work very diligently to bring all Christian pastors together in our city. Rick was a board member and writer for a Tucson Christian newspaper for six years. He helped to shape the purpose of the paper to be non-adversarial. Rick was selected out of a pool of over 600 pastors across the United States by the Rockefeller Foundation. Rick was the single selection to represent Christian pastors and ministries across the United States. This was a three year project. During that time he worked actively with Superior Court Judges, the Arizona head of fine arts, representatives of major businesses, state officials, and education. Currently, Rick is known in Arizona as a Pastor's Pastor. For ten years Rick helped to reshape a small adoption agency to a ministry that ministers to the needs of Children in Zambia.

He is currently the senior pastor of Connections AVC in Tucson, Arizona and believes that God is moving as powerfully as He had in the first century.

Introduction of the book

To be Kingdom oriented, we should be able to move in the variety of Gifts that God pours out. Imagine what it would be like to operate in gifts of the Holy Spirit, supernaturally touching the lives of people we meet. Think of how powerful ministry would be if we knew how to tap into the presence of God on a consistent basis. Paul compels us to learn about these "spiritual gifts." Why is this so important? These are gifts that God is making available for us to best represent Him. It is one of God's ways of bringing "Kingdom Breakthrough." It is also my position that since Paul divided the gifts of the Holy Spirit and the ministry gifts for clarity, so should we.

Several years ago I was at a conference in Baltimore. I hadn't seen my adult daughter and son-in-law for some time, so they drove up from Virginia Beach to have lunch with me. Our server was a very bubbly, efficient person who took care of our needs easily and quickly. God, though, began to show me details of her life. In a vision, I saw things that had happened to her that morning. I saw each of her seven children all crying hysterically, and I also saw her husband walk out of their marriage relationship to leave them with nothing.

I didn't say a word to my daughter or son-in-law, but when the server returned, I said, "Tell me about your seven children!" Then I said, "Your husband left you this morning and you don't know what is going to happen to you." She stood there dumbfounded. Finally, I said, "I am a pastor from Tucson, Arizona." She finished my sentence and said through her tears, "God sent you from Tucson to Baltimore to let me know that He still loves me!" She went away for a few minutes to refresh herself and when she returned I asked, "May I pray for you?"

So, what happened? I took the risk to believe and act on what I thought God was saying to me. This kind of ministry happens frequently with people who are open to God's gifts. When people are just learning to move in the gifts of the Spirit they frequently ask, "What if I am wrong?" You may ask the same question as you begin to explore. Actually, it is the wrong question. It should be, "What if I am right?" This attitude helps us to depend more on God and His gifts rather than on our own.

To move more easily in the spiritual gifts we will look at several areas, such as our individual design, selected gifts of the Holy Spirit, and "one time" gifts, or gifts that are granted for use in the moment of need. We will also tackle the question, "Does every person have gifts of the spirit available to them for the work of ministry?" "Do we each have a unique design (ministry) with gifts of the Holy Spirit that compliment that design?" Do the Holy Spirit gifts work independently of our ministry or divinely planned makeup? Could it be a mixture of both assigned gifts and gifts given for the ministry need?

In this study, I will use 1 Corinthians 12 as a starting point to look at what Paul called, (πνευματικων- *pneumatikon*) - spirituals. I have translated this "spiritual matters" or simply, gifts from God the Father, the Son and the Holy Spirit. In this study, I will follow the progression found in 1 Corinthians 12 and then graduate to Romans and Ephesians. I will follow this course with another course that addresses the "functions or ministries" that Jesus assigns to us.

There has been some discussion has to whether we "have" certain gifts or whether the Holy Spirit grants them when they are needed. I think that there is plenty of textual evidence to suggest that it isn't an either-or, but all inclusive. I believe that this position best fulfills John Wimber's, founder of the Community of Vineyard Churches, position on ministry: "Everyone can play." I intend to explore this at length.

Many of the stories are my own experiences. I do this so that those taking the course or listening to the lecture can see that they can relate to another person. These stories are not hypothetical, but have actually happened.

There will be a chapter for each gift of the Holy Spirit. The chapter will conclude with individual and group discussion. During this time the great question should be, "How can this gift move in my life today?"

Jeremiah 1:4-10 (NIV)

[4] The word of the LORD came to me, saying,

[5] "Before I formed you in the womb I knew you, before you were born I set you apart; I appointed you as a prophet to the nations."

[6] "Ah, Sovereign LORD," I said, "I do not know how to speak; I am only a child."

[7] But the LORD said to me, "Do not say, 'I am only a child.' You must go to everyone I send you to and say whatever I command you.

[8] Do not be afraid of them, for I am with you and will rescue you," declares the LORD.

[9] Then the LORD reached out his hand and touched my mouth and said to me, "Now, I have put my words in your mouth.

[10] See, today I appoint you over nations and kingdoms to uproot and tear down, to destroy and overthrow, to build and to plant."

Richard E Leis

Chapter one – the Divisions of the Spiritual Gifts

When Paul wrote the Corinthian church it was already operating in the Spiritual gifts. The problem was that they were still greatly influenced by their pre-Christian ways of doing things. This struggle continues as Paul addresses the use of the Spiritual gifts. God not only wants us to be informed about the gifts, but to operate in them in a balanced manner.[2]

Divisions of the Spiritual Gifts

Now there are diversities of gifts, but the same Spirit. And there are differences of administrations, but the same Lord. And there are diversities of operations, but it is the same God which worketh all in all. But the manifestation of the Spirit is given to every man to profit withal (1 Corinthians 12:4-7).

It is clear that Paul considers the Corinthians to be more "worldly" rather than spiritual or Godly.[3] Paul breaks down the Spirituals into three primary divisions. This progression gives a clear picture of how God works through us. If these divisions are recalled while reading the text, it makes it a lot easier to follow. Within 1 Corinthians 12 there are *gifts* from the Holy Spirit, *ministries* appointed by Jesus and *operations*

---

[2] Now about spiritual gifts, brothers, I do not want you to be ignorant (1 Corinthians 12:1).

[3] Brothers, I could not address you as spiritual but as worldly--mere infants in Christ (1 Corinthians 3:1).

from God. In some cases the gifts are mixed together. Paul uses this same progression or blend in his letters to the Ephesians and the Romans.

While God can and does supply a variety of gifts of the Holy Spirit on special occasions, it is not unusual to see "Gift Clusters." [4] Paul is telling the Corinthians to wake up and discover everything that they can about the spiritual gifts.

The Nine Gifts of the Spirit

First of all, Paul teaches about nine basic or core gifts of the Spirit. I believe that each gift can operate in an infinite number of ways because of God's infinite nature. For example, the gift of Working in Miracles doesn't just perform one creative event, but has the capacity to do any creative event that God chooses. In one instance a lost eye may be replaced, in another, a river may be parted and in another, seas calmed.

Ministry functions from Jesus

Imagine a fine piece of artwork. The artist had to imagine the finished product in his mind and maybe in his spirit. It is

---

[4] For you created my inmost being; you knit me together in my mother's womb. I praise you because I am fearfully and wonderfully made; your works are wonderful, I know that full well. My frame was not hidden from you when I was made in the secret place. When I was woven together in the depths of the earth, your eyes saw my unformed body. All the days ordained for me were written in your book before one of them came to be (Psalms 139:13-16 NIV).

often said of sculptors that they imagine an image in the stone before they make the first chisel mark.

I design and build electric basses and guitars. Prior to beginning the actual work, I decide on the basic shape. Many times I will design a new shape to fit a design in my mind's eye. Next, exotic woods are chosen, then I pick the hardware and neck design. [Since it is likely that true musicians may have long sets, I target specific light weights to fall within.] About forty to fifty hours later a fine instrument is finished. The truth of the matter is that even though a beautiful, fine crafted instrument has been created, it is only as good as the musician playing it.

Results Energized By God

Similarity, God designed us for a purpose (Psalm 139.13-16).[5] Just as I design my guitars, God carefully designs each of us. One of us may be a violin, a bass guitar, or a set of kettle drums. The gifts of the Holy Spirit are like the components and hardware that I add to my guitars. When we receive Christ, He awakens the ministry gifts in us; the gifts from the Holy Spirit complement those ministry gifts. It is like having a beautiful electric guitar hanging on the wall all set to make beautiful music. At that point it is simply a fine piece of wall art, but that all changes when the exceptional musician

---

[5] Results energized by God's grace (ἐνέργημα) though enérgema is translated "operations," it actually speaks to the results that have been energized by God's grace.

removes it from the wall, tunes the strings and then begins to play. Jesus does the same for us. When we commit our lives to Christ he then picks us up and begins to play us for the Father's glory. The Father, in a sense, is the amplifier through which the music is played. His grace energizes the results.

In addition to this, the Holy Spirit will assign gifts as they are needed. It could also be said that in any case, the gifts are not ours, but gifts to be used for God's purpose. To refine this further, Jesus assigns our ministry (purpose), the Holy Spirit compliments that ministry with his gifts, and the Father empowers the whole thing.

Paul's Focus for the Spiritual Gifts

The Corinthians had to be reminded that all of the spiritual gifts were given for the benefit of the entire body; they are not provided specifically for the blessing of any one individual. Paul makes it clear that these gifts do not make one Christian more important than another. The focus must always be on the giver rather than on the gift itself.[6]

Groupings of the Gifts of the Holy Spirit

I have seen the gifts grouped in a variety of ways, but ultimately they are broken down into three groups of three.

---

[6] 1 Corinthians 12.1-7

1. **THE GIFTS OF KNOWING** – They reveal part of God's knowledge.

2. **GIFTS OF DOING** – They are active, and do something.

3. **THE SPEAKING GIFTS** – They say something.

THESE THREE GROUPS CAN BE DESCRIBED IN A DIFFERENT WAY:

1. **GIFTS OF REVELATION** - They reveal something.

a. Gift of the word of knowledge.

b. Gift of the word of wisdom.

c. Gift of discerning of spirits.

2. **GIFTS OF POWER - THEY DO SOMETHING.**

a. Gift of faith

b. Gift of working of miracles

c. Gifts of healing.

3. **GIFTS OF UTTERANCE** - They say something.

a. Gift of prophecy.

b. Gift of speaking in different kinds of tongues.

c. Gift of interpretation of tongues.

None of the gifts of the Holy Spirit are enhancements of natural gifts. For instance, Discerning of spirits has little or no relationship to being discerning or intuitive. These spiritual gifts do not heighten natural gifts – the gifts of the Holy Spirit are supernatural or above the natural realm and are directly from God Himself.

For the sake of understanding each gift, I have separated them, but many of the gifts of the Spirit work together.

Group discussion

1. Name the nine gifts of the Spirit.

2. What is the goal of this course?

3. Does the author think that the gifts of the spirit are still in operation?

4. What are the three basic gifts of the Spirit?

Chapter 2 - The Gift of the Word of Knowledge

The gift of the word of knowledge is not embellished natural knowledge, but instead supplies us with knowledge from God about a person, from the present or the past. It could be said, that it is like one word out of the entire vocabulary of God. This gift provides just the right amount of information to minister to the person that you are drawn to.

Used in Outreach

Several California and Tucson Vineyards had joined together to have a "hands on" spiritual conference. Many of those in attendance were from non-charismatic churches. Following one of the afternoon sessions, I took a group of non-charismatic pastors to our largest indoor mall. The assignment was to allow the Holy Spirit to speak to us about someone in the mall and then go up to that person and minister to them. My pastor friends were gulping by the time we got to the mall. This was way outside their experience and belief, although all of them were willing to try it at least once.

Let's Pray

We walked the bottom floor of the mall and really didn't sense anything. At one point I sat down, and felt like the Holy Spirit was guiding us to the opposite end of the mall. We walked there and then I said, "Let's pray and see if God points out a particular person, and gives us information about them as well."[7]

As we began to pray as a group, I looked up and there was a young woman selling "Lo Jack" or a locator device to find an automobile when it is stolen. While my pastor friends were praying I began to get information about this woman, her daughter and boyfriend. I then shared with the other pastors the Word of Knowledge that I had received about this young saleswoman.

She had a six year old daughter, and was afraid for her safety. Her boyfriend had been dealing drugs, his case recently went to trial and he was found guilty. The Holy Spirit also showed me that the boyfriend was now in prison in Douglas, Arizona. My pastor friends gave me a variety of looks ranging from wow to the ultimate skeptic. My instruction to the pastors was to follow me over and just pretend like they were interested in the car. I engaged the young woman in conversation, and then said, "Your boyfriend is in prison in Douglas, and you are worried about what is going to happen to you and your six year old daughter." As soon as I mentioned these things I had her attention. "How do you know these things?" "I am a

---

[7] When teaching others how to be open to the gifts of the Spirit, it is important to begin with prayer. It helps to focus everyone on God's answer.

pastor, and I was sitting over there praying for you and God told me about you, may I pray for you." She said, "I don't know, I am Catholic." Several years prior, I had begun praying with the Bishop of Tucson, so I said, "the Bishop is one of my prayer partners, and if he lets me pray with him don't you suppose that I can pray for you as well?" It was in those few moments that she saw that God was looking out for both her and her daughter. I saw things about her past and present. There was no other way that I could possibly know anything about her, unless I had seen her personal diary.

A Gift from God

This is a gift from God, it is not all of God's knowledge, and it is not a gift of knowledge or a natural gift that makes the person's recall of historic information better.

Following our trip to Tucson mall, the pastors agreed that what they had witnessed was indeed a supernatural revelation from the Holy Spirit. Since we did not know everything about the young women, it was just a fragment of God's knowledge. It was exactly what we needed to minister to her. She needed to know that God was watching out for her, she was not alone. She needed to know that her daughter would be alright. The information only covered past and present information or events in this woman's life.

Pastor's Conference

Several years ago, I was one of the presiding pastors over Southwest Minister's Conference. This included Charismatic pastors from Oregon to Mexico. We usually had between 800 – 1,000 pastors and their wives in attendance. At the end of our evening sessions we always had ministry time where we were open to the move of God's gifts. It's usual that one of us on the pastoral team would hear from the Holy Spirit about some malady. For example we would then announce it by saying, "God is healing someone with TMJ, lower back, cancer and so on."

While it is true that if you announce an illness while in a large assembly of people, it is likely that at least one will respond. That is true, but when they are healed because you have been obedient, it really doesn't matter what others have to say. My rule of thumb is not to let negative people prevent the Holy Spirit from moving.

A Pastor with TMJ

After one of these sessions the Holy Spirit told me that there was "one" person in the crowd that suffered from debilitating pain in their jaw (TMJ). There were several who stood in their place, I prayed for their healing and then I asked them to sit down. The next morning I was in the church bookstore and I heard a shout for joy, and this Mexican pastor literally tackled me shouting that he was healed. This pastor could no longer speak without pain, and eating was full of agony as well. He kept shouting, "Jesus has healed me. I was so depressed I was going to quit the ministry."

Biblical Examples:

John, writing to the seven churches in the province of Asia: Grace and peace to you from him who is, and who was, and who is to come, and from the seven spirits before his throne (Revelation 1:4). John is a prisoner on the small rocky Isle of Patmos; he has no communication with the churches in Asia. All knowledge that he has of the churches is supplied by the Holy Spirit through the gift of the Word of Knowledge. Other gifts that are active at the same time are the gift of the word of wisdom.[8]

[8] I, John, your brother and companion in the suffering and kingdom and patient endurance that are ours in Jesus, was on the island of Patmos because of the word of God and the testimony of Jesus. On the Lord's Day I was in the Spirit, and I heard behind me a loud voice like a trumpet, which said: "Write on a scroll what you see and send it to the seven churches: to Ephesus, Smyrna, Pergamum, Thyatira, Sardis, Philadelphia and Laodicea" (Revelation 1:9-11).

GROUP WORK

Study Revelation 1.1 - 3:22

List the things that the Holy Spirit reveals about things past and present:

1.

2.

3.

Ananias and Paul

Acts 9:10-16

1. Study the interaction between the Holy Spirit, Ananias and Paul.

2. List the things that the Holy Spirit reveals about things present and past.

3. If the revelation of future facts and events is the gift of the word of Wisdom, the revelation of present and past facts and events is the gift of the word of Knowledge, identify those gifts in these passages.

4. How do the lines between these gifts become blurred?

Chapter 3 -   The gift of the word of Wisdom

Paul wanted the Corinthians to understand the nature and purpose of the Gifts of the Spirit. He also reminded them that the Holy Spirit Himself determines who gets what gift mix and the end result would be for the common good.[9]   The gifts of revelation are the gift of the word of knowledge, the gift of the word of wisdom, and the gift of discerning of spirits. None of these gifts are personal possessions, but are for the entire body of Christ. They do not belong to any one individual. These are gifts rooted in the divine nature of God and have nothing to do with natural gifts of *knowledge, wisdom or discernment.*

Revelation of God's divine will

The gift of the word of wisdom reveals God's divine will and purpose in the present or future. It also reveals facts about places, people or events in the future. God doesn't reveal all of the facts; He just reveals the ones that He wants us to know. The gift of the Word of Wisdom and the gift of the Word of Knowledge frequently work together. It is like having one

---

[9] 1 Corinthians 12.7

word about the present or future out of the entire vocabulary of God. To the Apostle John, God reveals the present, past and future of the Seven Churches; this is a classic example of the operation of the gift of the word of wisdom (*Revelation 1:9-12)*. John said, "On the Lord's Day I was in the spirit, and I heard behind me a loud voice . . . (1.10).

Jesus

Jesus appeared to John either in a vision or he was actually taken into the presence of God. Either way, the Holy Spirit revealed facts past, present and future about the seven churches in Asia Minor. While it was possible for John to have information from the past, it was not possible for John to know the current and future events of the churches in Asia Minor because he was a prisoner. The purpose of John's revelation was to draw the churches back to Godliness. John identified the past history of each church, talked about their strengths and then warned them of God's judgment upon them. Each church had the opportunity to change and return to their first love (Christ). It was the direction of the church and its resulting judgment that would be revealed by the gift of the word of wisdom.

"I am fertile!"

One Sunday morning our service was packed out. There were just a few seats left up front. A childless young couple arrived late and ended up sitting on the front row. The couple wanted children very badly, but had gone barren for many years. As is the case with many childless couples, their sadness was almost overwhelming. During my sermon, the Holy Spirit began to speak with me about their future. I saw in a vision, many children in their family. The Lord had me stop right in the middle of my sermon, have the couple stand, then turn and face the congregation and announce, "I am fertile." The congregation loved this couple and they broke out with shouts of joy and exuberant clapping. Before the entire congregation, I said to the couple, "You are not just getting one child, but you are going to have three." It is some years later, and they have three beautiful children.

Hysterectomy and the promise of 6 children

On another occasion, a close friend of ours, who was an executive at the local college, really wanted a husband and children. The men in her life were all intimidated by her position with the college and so were afraid to date her. One evening Marilyn, my wife, and I were praying for our friend and I got this word. "In six months' time you will be married, and you and your husband will have six children." The following month she had a hysterectomy. I thought to myself, "Well, I guess I blew that 'word.'" Following her recovery she decided to go on a historic Luther Lands tour. While on the tour she met a gentleman who was the president of two oil companies. He was not intimidated by her job or position.

He was on the tour because his wife had been ill, tripped and hit her head on the coffee table, and was killed. Six weeks after they returned from the tour, they were married. Oh! I forgot to mention. He had six children ranging from a few months to early teens. Imagine what would have happened had I not taken the risk to say something to our friend?

How may I hear the Holy Spirit?

None of us hear God exactly the same way, but there are some basic ways that God does speak to us. All of these ways are dependent on our own intimacy with Him by studying his word, and through prayer. Those are important because we become familiar with the presence of God and his words to us.

I will just touch on the ways we might hear God, but cover the subject later in this course. You could rightly say that there are infinite ways to hear God. The most common are through dreams, visions, actual voice, an inner voice, prophecy, tongues and interpretation. Often when I minister to people I see vivid, movies or visions, which is very much like an open eye dream.

The Dream that persists

Audrey Langdon, in her book, *Dreams, Visions, and Spiritual Messages* says, "The dream that persists, capturing the conscious brain, is a different matter. Such dreams have had a dramatic impact on individual lives, and at times on the course of human history. One of the best known examples is the Biblical patriarch Joseph, who became an exile and slave after telling his brothers about a dream that prophesied they would bow down to him. Through his ability to interpret other peoples' dreams he eventually became the prime minister of Egypt, saving the nation from devastation or famine, and simultaneously saving the lives of his bothers, who did bow down, unknowingly to him.[10] Joseph operated in the gift of the word of wisdom which manifested in his dreams.

Visions – Ananias and Paul

Following Paul's conversion experience on the way to Damascus, the Lord came to Ananias and told him exactly where Paul was. At the same time Paul was seeing Ananias in a vision coming to him to place his hands on him to restore his sight. The Lord also told Ananias that Paul was his chosen instrument to "carry His name before the Gentiles…" God provided specific information so that Ananias could find Paul. He also gave him very specific instructions for what he was to do when he met him. God also provide Ananias the details of Paul's conversion. This would be a confirmation to Paul that God was working in his life. With a touch, Paul's sight was restored (Acts 9:10-19).

---

[10] *Dreams, Visions, and Spiritual Messages,* Audrey Langdon, J.&J Publishers-Falls Church, Virginia pg 5

Joseph and Dreams

Joseph had a dream, and when he told it to his brothers, they hated him all the more (Genesis 37:5).

God spoke to Joseph as a young boy in dreams. The dreams showed that at some point in his future, his family, including his parents, would bow down to him because of his rank or station. Joseph's brothers were jealous of him after their father gave Jacob gave Joseph the robe of many colours. Joseph not only remembered his dreams but acted on them.

What Paul would later call the "gift of the word of wisdom" was evident in a series of dreams. They told of a future truth in the lives of Joseph, his family and Egypt.

Should Joseph have shared his dreams? Would that have changed his future or made things easier? We can only speculate about that. What did happen was that God provided the faith and encouragement to walk through some very difficult times. In the end, he rescued the children of Israel from a great famine through Joseph.

Agabus the Prophet – Famine

27 During this time some prophets came down from Jerusalem to Antioch.

28 One of them, named Agabus, stood up and through the Spirit

predicted that a severe famine would spread over the entire Roman world. (This happened during the reign of Claudius.)
[29] The disciples, each according to his ability, decided to provide help for the brothers living in Judea.
[30] This they did, sending their gift to the elders by Barnabas and Saul (Acts 11:27-30)

.

The text does not say how Agabus saw into the future, it does say that through the Spirit Agabus predicted a sever famine throughout the Roman Empire.   This forewarning allowed the Church to respond to the human catastrophe that would come. It is possible that Agabus had a dream or vision prior to his coming to Antioch.   It could also be true that he had a prophetic word while in the service at Antioch.   It isn't important to know which method of communication that the Holy Spirit used.   What is important is that Agabus did hear and respond to the leadership of the Holy Spirit. Through Agabus, the church heard that the famine would spread throughout the Roman Empire and they began preparing for the victims of the famine.

Agabus binds Paul

After several days of visiting, a prophet from Judea by the name of Agabus came down to see us (21.10).

Paul and his troupe stopped for a few days rest in Caesarea in Philip the apostles' home. Once again, the prophet Agabus brings a word about Paul's future. He has seen Paul bound up in Jerusalem. There are those who are intent on killing Paul. His friends assumed that since Paul would be captured and bound, it would be a bad thing. Dramatically Agabus ties Paul's hands and feet. His disciples wanted Paul to avoid Jerusalem, but instead Paul responded, "That obviously is not God's will for me." [11]"You're looking at this backwards. The issue in Jerusalem is not what they do to me, whether arrest or murder, but what the Master does through my obedience." Just because Agabus brought a word about Paul's future, Paul didn't change his plans. He knew that he was to take the Good News of Christ to the gentiles. I think when we receive dreams or words of wisdom; we need to ask God what he wants us to do with it. Paul shows an important principle in operating in the gifts of the Spirit. There will be times when people have a "word" for you, they may even pressure you to follow "God's will" but you feel "in your spirit" that the advice they give as an interpretation is not correct.

YOUNG COUPLE – FALSE WORD

There was a young newly engaged couple in our church that had heard that the Holy Spirit was really moving in a church in San Diego. They were also new in their relationship with

---

[11] Acts 21.12-14

Christ and very new to the "Charismatic gifts." For the sake of the story, I'll call her Beth.

When the couple first walked into the service of the San Diego Church, the senior pastor was quite attracted to her and one of his elders stood in front of the church and declared, "Verily, verily, thus says the Lord, Beth is to marry our pastor." The couple returned very confused, he was hurt and she didn't want to go against God's will. After several weeks of counselling, the couple finally broke up and left the church. It was a very sad situation. Despite the fact that our staff counselled them and encouraged them to put it behind themselves, they could not.

Just because someone purports to represent God, it doesn't mean that they always do. One rule to use when trying to decide if this was actually God or not is to ask the question, "Does this match the nature and character of God?" "Does it go against the nature and character of Scripture?"

AUDIBLE VOICE – HEZEKIAH

Hezekiah had become quite sick and was close to death. God spoke to Isaiah and said to proclaim over Hezekiah that he was to "get his house in order" because his death was to be immediate. Isaiah's pronouncement that Hezekiah was going to die and not recover was the gift of the word of wisdom.

Hezekiah's reaction was immediate. While in his bed, he turned his face to the wall and cried out, "Remember me, O Lord, how I have walked before you faithfully . . . [12]

Just as Isaiah was walking through the middle courtyard of the palace, God spoke to him again and said, "Go back and tell Hezekiah that I have heard his prayers of how he was been wholeheartedly devote and done what was good in my sight. Tell Hezekiah that I have added fifteen years to his life." God also promised to protect the city from that Assyrians and to defend the city for the sake of David. Isaiah prepared a poultice of figs, the boils were covered and he recovered. Isaiah was also shown by God to make the poultice. This once again is the gift of the word of wisdom.[13]

DEBILITATING CLUSTER HEADACHES

There was a woman in our church that had debilitating cluster[14] type headaches much of her life. As a church and individually we had prayed for her many times and nothing seemed to improve. Her husband works at the University of Arizona and called me late one afternoon and said, "Danielle is having those headaches again and it is really bad, would you please

---

[12] 2 Kings 20.2-3

[13] 2 Kings 20.4-7

[14] Cluster headaches are excruciating unilateral headaches [1] of extreme intensity.[2] The duration of the http://en.wikipedia.org/wiki/Cluster_headache common attack ranges from as short as 15 minutes to three hours or more.

come out to my house and pray for her?" I agreed to meet Charlie at their home, which was about 80 minutes from my office. Charlie is a real stable man, and he sounded panic stricken. To be truthful, I did not want to go pray for her once again without her being healed. I got in my car, and said to the Lord, "I am not going to start this car until you show me what to do for her healing." I heard these words, "pour salt into her hand." That was it.

Pour salt into her hand

I started up the car and headed for their home. When I got there, an adult daughter greeted me at the door. She had decided to move in with her parents until she got situated in Tucson. She had also terminated a relationship that was not good for her. Charlie arrived about the same time I did. He said, "What are you going to do?" I said, "Let's go into the bedroom and greet Danielle." He went back to prepare his wife and then called the daughter and I. Charlie said, "Well, let's pray." I replied, "Charlie, I prayed for direction from God before I left the office. I am not going to pray. I am going to pour salt into her hand. Charlie is the scientist type, so he said, "What kind of salt?" "Do you want Kosher salt, sea salt...I said, "Charlie, God didn't say, just bring the one you like." I explained what God told me to do to Danielle, and then I asked for her hand. I poured salt into her hand and she kept it there.

Finally, Danielle asked if we could have communion. The only kind of juice they had was V-8. So we had communion with that. The daughter refused to take communion with us because she was upset that Danielle was not healed on the spot. She was still hurting very badly from seeing no action on God's part.

"Pastor Rick, Danielle is totally healed from her headache!"

I received a call from Charlie the next morning. "Pastor Rick, Danielle is totally healed from her headaches." Now it is several years later and they have not returned. The daughter recommitted her life to Christ. She had walked away from God when she was a little child because God didn't answer her prayers for her mom. Several gifts were in operation in her, but the direction to pour salt in her had would fall under the category of the gift of the word of wisdom.

Group Study:

1. Study the book of Jonah to find the gift of the Word of Knowledge and the gift of the Word of Wisdom.

List other examples of both gifts from the book of Jonah

2. What other examples can you find of these gifts in the Old Testament?

Study Philip in Acts, chapter 8.

1. List out the manner in which the Gifts of the Word of Knowledge and Wisdom work in Philip's life.

 2. How might God use this gift in your life?

ACTS 27.10FF   (PAUL IS DELIVERED FROM A STORM)

1. How might God do this for you?

2. What does this study tell you about God and the Church?

IN THE ABOVE TEXT:

3. Pick out examples of the gift of the Word of Knowledge?

4. Pick out examples of the gift of the word of wisdom.

What do you think?

1. In what ways might we receive the gift of the Word of Knowledge or the gift of the Word of Wisdom?

The Gift of Discerning of Spirits   Chapter 4

Definition:

The gift of the discerning of spirits gives godly insight into the spirit world. It is not solely the perception of demons nor is it solely the gift of discerning good spirits. The gift of discerning of spirits perceives both godly and ungodly spirits and it grants some insight into the spirit world. It does not grant total insight into the spirit world.

Satan is alive and well!

Shortly after committing my life to Christ, I had to make a decision as to whether I would go back into ministry or give our very successful business my full attention. At the time I had a husky, black and white male cat that never left my side. There was an easy chair by my side of the bed and that was where Rocky slept.   About 2.00 am I woke with a start and standing at the foot of our bed was an expensively dressed businessman (Satan) telling me to follow him and he would give me riches and success. There were also demon faces flashing on and off around his head. I was horrified. I looked over at my wife and she was quietly sleeping, I looked at Rocky and he was fast asleep. The fear kept mounting so I could hardly speak.

Hale Lindsey had just come out with a book about demons, so I thought, "What did Hall Lindsey say in his book to get rid of demons?"[15] I croaked out the formula prayer, "Satan I command you out of my house and away from my family" and nothing happen. It seemed like Satan and his minions were getting closer. I cried out in my mind, "God, help me!" A quiet but powerful voice said to me, "Rick, what did I say?" I looked at Satan and the demons circle around his head who were flashing on and off. I shouted out, "Satan and your demons I command you in the name of Jesus to get out of my house!" They began to move backwards as if down a long tube, and then I began to laugh. With the laughter, Satan and the demons disappeared. I was wide awake; I looked at my wife and then touched her. She continued to sleep as did Rocky. I was so much at peace that I was able to go right to sleep. I learned that God's word is powerful; not someone who is suggesting formula prayers for all occasions.

This gift of discerning of spirits helped me to see who was coming against me. It was the Lord himself that contended with Satan.

Isaiah and his view of the heavenlies

Isaiah said that after king Uzziah died he was transported to heaven and was able to observe the Lord (Isaiah 6.1-4). Later, the apostle John had a similar experience, and was translated

---

[15] Satan is Alive and Well on Planet Earth, Zondervan, Hal Lindsey

into the presence of God. I believe the gift of discerning of spirits enabled them to see the Lord and the Seraphs. Scripture really does not tell us how he was able to see into the Spirit dimension. It could have been a dream, a vision, but most likely he was taken into the presence of the Lord and His Temple.

This gift is experienced in a variety of ways. Some people literally have the hair on their bodies stand up on end when they go into a business, home or some other location that is demonic influenced. Others have a real deep sense of peace. This is the Holy Spirit telling you that you are in the presence of good or evil.

"Water, I want water!"

We did all of our logistics from a very large, beautiful meeting room complete with a glass wall to the outside and a huge flagstone fireplace. The room itself held about 300 people. As a Lutheran, I was in charge of the young adults. On this one particular night we had about fifteen teams and we set out to visit the non-attending youth of our church.

Our team got its assignments and we left to go visit with the missing young people. About three hours later we returned to the "fireside room." It was packed, but all of the people had their backs to the glass wall. It was almost like a bunch of cattle with their back side to the wind. I looked outside and there was a man dressed in a robe, head covered, feet in sandals and he carried a staff. This was not unusual for Santa Barbara; we had all kinds of strange people populate the area. The man was mouthing, "water, I want water." I asked the crowd why they didn't serve him, and they said that they were afraid, all 300 of them.

A glass of water

I told him to wait, and went down to our kitchen and got him a glass of cold water. I wasn't afraid; I just took two really big guys with me. When I got outside we were directly in front of the glass wall. All three hundred people were watching us hand this rather strange person a glass of water. He quickly drank it down, handed the glass to me and said, "thank you." As he was walking away, I felt compelled to shout out, "Shalom!" He turned, looked me right in the eyes, lifted his staff and said, "Shalom! Shalom!" One second he was there and the next he was not. The entire outreach crowd of people saw this and some were "wowed" by the experience, others were just stunned. We had all seen the angel first hand. That was the gift of discerning of spirits.

Singing Angels

At the time, I was president of the Full Gospel Businessmen in Santa Barbara. I had invited the sons of Demos Shakarian, the president of Full Gospel Businessmen to do a fund raiser to help troubled youth.[16] Prior to the fundraiser we served dinner to about 600 businessmen from the community. Right in the middle of the prayer, the bar band, in another room, started up and it was loud even though the doors were closed. I was grumbling to the Lord about it when the music changed to the most beautiful music I have ever heard. I opened my eyes, and stationed all around the room were massive, strong, golden angels. Their wings touched in the middle of the room as if they had formed a protective canopy over us. The music I heard was their singing. I closed my eyes again and when I looked up they were no longer visible.

For those few moments in time, I was able to see into the spirit dimension.

While there are a number of gifts of the spirit all working together, the gift Discerning of spirits allowed the Apostle John to see into the God dimension (Revelation 1.1-3). Dr. Paul Yonggi Cho calls this the 4th Dimension, or a place where we can freely communicate with God. Dr. Cho says, "God originally created us as physical beings. Yet, having breathed the breath of life into Adam, He gave him the capacity to understand and communicate with God in another than the physical level. He could communicate in the dimension of

---

[16] Founder of The Full Gospel Businessmen

Spirit. 'God is a Spirit. [17]Those that worship God must worship Him in Spirit and truth.'" (John 4.24) John was moved by the gift of Discerning of spirits. He saw into the spirit dimension. We could call it the Fourth Dimension.

Missionary sees into the Spirit world

Prior to becoming a pastor, I was attending our Lutheran service with my wife and children. Pastor Gene Bunkowsky, a missionary from Nigeria was introduced to the congregation. After the service, he came up to me and told me that the Holy Spirit told him to come see me and I would give him what he needed. He said that my name was known in Africa as one who would pray for spiritual gifts and people would get results. I didn't know how this could possibly be, because I had only been moving in the gifts about two months. Gene ministered to the Yala Tribe in Nigeria.[18] No individual could be part of the Water Society"[19] with its power and status unless they sacrificed their oldest child to the demons. At sunset the person was put into the hut of sacrifice and by sunrise the next morning they were dead. No one saw a demon, but they could feel the presence of demons, and the proof lay in the hut.[20]

---

[17] The Fourth Dimension - Volume Two, Paul Yonggi Cho, Bridge Publishing, pg xi

[18] The Yala people numbered around 150,000

[19] The most influential social and political group among the Yala

[20] Lutheran Bible Translators – Gene Bunkowsky

Pastor Gene Bunkowsky, a Lutheran Bible Translator,[21] was praying about ways to reach the chief and witch doctor. These were the two most powerful men in the tribe. One afternoon, Gene was walking along a dirt path to his hut when a cow gored him in the gut. This was a wound that could have been fatal as it penetrated his intestines. The Lord spoke to Gene and said, "Go lay down in your hut and I will heal you."

Word got out because this was a direct confrontation between two spiritual worlds.[22] Gene was healed, the chief gave his life to Christ and so did the native doctor. The native doctor still had not sent his oldest to the demon hut.[23] The rule was that if you did not sacrifice your oldest child, then you were required to be the substitute and go into the demon hut yourself. At sunset the native doctor walked into the hut. He experienced God warring against evil. At sunrise, the native doctor walked out of the demon hut unharmed. The result of this was that most of the tribe (150,000) people invited Christ into their lives. The people saw that God was more powerful that the evil spirits that they had worshipped. The gift of discerning of spirits manifested when it allowed Gene, the

---

[21] LBY: Our mission is to help bring people to faith in Jesus Christ by making the Word of God available to those who do not yet have it in the language of their hearts.

[22] Good and Evil, Godly and ungodly.

[23] *The Water Society* required the sacrifice of the oldest child. It provided spiritual and political clout.

chief and native doctor to feel the presence of God more than the threat of the demons.

Prayer walking

Joe, my closest pastor friend called me up and said, "Rick, there is some heavy duty demonic activity fairly close to my church. "Would you please come join me in praying against these demons?"

In Tucson, we have huge dry river beds called "washes." Connected to these washes is a system of drainage pipes that are large enough to walk upright in and they run extensively under our city. In this one area, we found occult altars and witchcraft and demonic signs painted all throughout these tunnels. About thirty to forty feet above there was a very large overpass.

There were a number of tunnels that went for miles back into the neighbourhoods. As we approached an area that had been marked with a number of Satanic symbols, I saw a large number of demonic beings running and hiding from us. Every few seconds they would peek out at us and then just take off. The hair stood up on the back of my neck and on my arms.

Suddenly Joe started laughing. While I saw the demonic enemy running, he saw a huge angel standing directly behind us. The angel was so large that only his feet and ankles could be seen under the underpass. The demons were not running from us, but from the one who God sent to protect us as we prayed.[24]

Gauging the spirit

In addition to working in the gifts of the Spirit there are also other ways for measuring which spirit you are dealing with.

Know the word of God

Rather than base your impression of the presence of God upon feelings alone, it is important that those wishing to move in the gifts of the Spirit, know the Word of God and know his voice as well. [25] I consistently tell our classes, if you take the Word of God out of context, it is no longer the word of God. Don't just grab a bunch of verses to make them say something they do not, but instead look at the whole story and then interpret what it says. The more frequently we read the words of Christ, the deeper those words go into our being. Consequently when the wrong spirit comes along and quotes Scripture out of context we know that it is not God.

---

[24] Large wash under Ina Road in Tucson

[25] **Romans 10:17 (NIV)**

[17] Consequently, faith comes from hearing the message, and the message is heard through the word of Christ.

Listen to the Holy Spirit

As we pray and read the word, God will make himself known to us. The Holy Spirit will come and remind us of all of the things that He has told us (John 14.26)

Ask, "Does it reflect the nature and character of Christ?"

Review: What is the gift of discerning of spirits?

When the gifts of the Spirit are claimed to have ceased in the first century, then those who purport that position cannot see the gifts as supernatural ones from God.[26] Therefore this supernatural gift becomes a gift of discernment or just heightened human gifting. This is not some form of psychological insight, the ability to read someone's thoughts nor is it fault finding. So then, what is it? It is a gift rooted in God and not in us. It is supernatural. Either it is "knowing" whether the spirit in question is divine, evil or simply from the human spirit. Some cases of mental illness are spiritual, others are genetic, and others are the result of an accident, drugs, or a variety of things. The gift of discerning of spirits allows us to minister to the people who are suffering from demonic affliction. The gifts of word of knowledge and

---

[26] Cessationism - All supernatural gifts stopped when the Canon of Scripture was complete.

wisdom help us to operate in the gift of miracles or the gifts of healing. God will not say, "Use the gift of . . ."

Steps to follow

If, while ministering to people, you are not sure what is behind the person's malady, go to the Holy Spirit and ask Him to show you what is going on. The gift of Discerning of spirits will enable you to see the Godly or ungodly spirits working around or in the person. When ministering to people don't focus on the faults that you see in the person, but rather ask the Holy Spirit to reveal the spirit behind the problem and pray for that.

Paul's encounter with the fortune teller Acts 16.16-20.

16 Once when we were going to the place of prayer, we were met by a slave girl who had a spirit by which she predicted the future. She earned a great deal of money for her owners by fortune-telling. 17 This girl followed Paul and the rest of us, shouting, "These men are servants of the Most High God, who are telling you the way to be saved." (Acts 16:16-17).

I have translated this text from the Greek and used the same terms found in there.

"It came to pass when we were going to the place of prayer, a certain maid servant who had a Python Spirit[27] (Spirit of Apollo), was bringing a great deal of business to her masters by telling fortunes. This girl followed Paul and the rest of us shouting, 'These men are servants of the most High God, who are telling you a way to be saved."[28]

With a clearer translation, it is easier to see why Paul responded so adamantly. He sensed Satan operating in the girl under the guise of the Python Spirit or the Spirit of Apollo. The young girl was announcing that Paul was preaching about "a way" of Salvation or one among many.

I don't know what I am doing here either!!!!

I had just finished giving an altar call for people to receive the "baptism" in the Holy Spirit. [29] As I recall, there were eight to nine hundred people that responded. There were three of us pastors laying hands on people and then praying for their "baptism." I had prayed for about 150 people and I came upon a young man. As soon as I put my hand on him to pray, the Holy Spirit said to me, "he is not saved!" So I looked him in the eyes and said, "You are not saved!" and he replied,

---

[27] πύθων - *Python spirit of divination in the ancient Greek world. Sometimes referred to as the Spirit of Apollo.*

[28] *The Complete Biblical Library, Springfield, Missouri ,Ps 388-389*

[29] In those days, the baptism of the Holy Spirit meant that someone began speaking in tongues when prayed for.

"And I don't know what I am doing here either." He then ran out of the building. I grieved for him, I kept asking myself, "How could I have done this differently?" "I ran him off!" A few evenings later, I was preparing to teach in our School of the Bible, and the same person walked into my office. He said, "Pastor, I came to give my life to Christ. Only God could have known that I was not a Christian, and you picked me out of a huge crowd." That evening he invited Jesus into his life.

Group Discussion

1. Of the gifts that we have studied so far, which ones are evident in this lesson?

2. Have you been trying to use some of them in ministry? Does your church?

3. Form groups of three or four and pray that God will flood you with his gifts.

Now ask the Holy Spirit to use the gifts that you have studied in one another and now minister to one person at a time in your group.

Allow the Holy Spirit to work through you. Later, identify which gifts you have been operating in.

The Gift of Faith - Chapter 5

Power Gifts: Gift of faith, working of miracles and gifts of healing

We might call these three gifts the action gifts. In my opinion, the gift of faith is the most important of the three power gifts. This is not a fruit of the Spirit which is provided to develop Christ-like behaviour. It is not every day trust in God which is developed by the continuous hearing of the true word of God.[30]

Consequently, faith comes from hearing the message (Gospel message), and the message is heard through the word of Christ (Romans 10:17)

God provides this gift so that we are able to believe that God will accomplish his supernatural work. For instance, if God was to tell me to make a poultice of spit and dirt, rub it on the face of a blind man and then he would be healed, God would also give me the faith to believe that He would return sight of the blind man if I followed his directions.

Daniel and the Lion's Den

"My God sent his angel and he shut the mouths of the lions. They have not hurt me, because I was found innocent in his sight. Nor have I ever done any wrong before you, O king"*(Daniel 6:22)*.

---

[30] True word – Scripture that is kept within the context in which it is written.

I think that we can be reasonably sure that Daniel was able to see the angel protecting him from the lions. God's assurance began with King Darius, "May your God, whom you serve continually, rescue you!"[31]

Secondly, God used the means that would bring assurance to Daniel. He saw the angels protecting him and he recalled throughout the night the wonders that God had done in his lifetime. God supplied the faith for Daniel to believe that He would protect him. This is very similar to King Nebuchadnezzar throwing Shadrach, Meshach, and Abednego into the fiery furnace.[32] God supplied the faith for them to believe that He would rescue them.

Gideon and the Angel of the Lord

God provides whatever we need to trust Him to fulfil His own word.

The angel of the LORD came and sat down under the oak in Ophrah that belonged to Joash the Abiezrite, where his son Gideon was threshing wheat in a winepress to keep it from the Midianites. [12] When the angel of the LORD appeared to Gideon, he said, "The LORD is with you, mighty warrior." (Judges 6.12-13)

---

[31] Daniel 6.6
[32] Daniel 3.16-18

While this is the angel of the Lord, God still had to make him visible so that Gideon could see and relate to him. Gideon had to perceive that this was an Angelic of God. With his very first words, the angel of the Lord names Gideon. "The Lord is with you mighty warrior (6.13)." Following a few questions, the angel of the Lord says, "Go in the strength you have and save Israel out of Midian's hand (6.14). Gideon asks question after question until he understands that the Lord Himself will be with him. This process builds faith in Gideon to trust that whatever God assigns him, no matter how impossible it looks; God is with him (Judges 6.19).

Finally, Gideon prepared a meal for the angel of God. The angel then instructed him to take the meat and unleavened bread that he had prepared and place the meal on a specific rock.

21 with the tip of the staff that was in his hand, the angel of the LORD touched the meat and the unleavened bread. Fire flared from the rock, consuming the meat and the bread (Judges 6.22).

Following that Gideon declares, "*Ah, Sovereign Lord! I have seen the angel of the Lord face to face*" (6.28).

Each step of the way, the Angel of the Lord took time to build Gideon's trust or faith in him. Gideon was selected by God as a result of Israel crying out to God in repentance. We learn from Gideon's example that when we are given Godly assignments, He will give us the faith to believe that God will do exactly what He has promised.

Jesus and the Storm

When using Jesus as an example we have to be careful to remember that he operated in the same gifts that are available to us. He did not act out of His divinity. Jesus had to be totally man to usher in the Kingdom of God.

Jesus was asleep in the boat when the storm hit. The disciples were afraid that they were going to die, that the storm would sink their boat. They began to cry out to Jesus, "Wake up or we are going to die." [26] He replied, "You of little faith, why are you so afraid?" Then he got up and rebuked the winds and the waves, and it was completely calm. [27] The men were amazed and asked, *"What kind of man is this? Even the winds and the waves obey him Matthew - 8:26-27 (NIV)*

Jesus knew that he had a purpose for his life and it was not fulfilled, therefore God would not let him die in the sea. When Jesus said to his disciples, "You of little faith, why are you so afraid?" he was saying, "Don't you get it?" Jesus' operated in the gift of faith and believed that his Father would calm the storm when Jesus rebuked the storm. Jesus was not someone who snuck up on God and said, "Well, maybe, when you have time, would you please stop the storm?" He shouted a command, "Storm, be still!" It was the gift of faith in action in Jesus. He had no doubt that God would perform it.

Deaf and Mute

Bill, an amazing twenty seven year old missionary to India believes that the best way to bring the Kingdom of God into people's lives is through "Power Evangelism."[33] Bill is not his real name but I use it to protect his ministry in India. Bill is very fluent in Hindi, he is able to read and write it fluently.

While riding in a rickety, old van he saw two men sitting on a grassy highway divider. He yelled out to the driver, "Pull over. Stop now!" He had noticed one of the two men signing. God gave him the faith to believe that if he prayed for the men, they would be healed. Bill ran back to the two men and tried to engage them in conversation. The men didn't understand because of their deafness. Bill then went to the first man and made signs that he wanted to pray for him. In the Indian culture they lose face if they turn you down. So the gentleman nodded his head "yes."

---

[33] Power Evangelism, John Wimber and Kevin Springer – Harper San Francisco - 1992

Bill stuck his fingers in the man's ears, all the while getting puzzled looks from the deaf man. He was led to command the spirit of deafness out of this man. He took his fingers out of the man's ears and he was no longer deaf. He then commanded the "mute" spirit out of the man. This man was deaf and mute from birth. He could hear and then Bill had him repeat some simple words.

Something similar happened to the second man. Bill had to pray and contend more for the second man, but eventually he was able to hear. Both men were literate, that is they could read and write. Bill invited them to his crusade that evening. They showed up at the meeting with 30 other deaf and mute friends. Today, the two are thriving Christians and are influential in expanding the Kingdom of God in Northern India. This type of thing is very usual for Bill. He teaches "The best way to evangelize is through miracles."

Isaac Blesses Jacob

Genesis 27:28-29

[28] *May God give you of heaven's dew and of earth's richness-- an abundance of grain and new wine.* [29] *May nations serve you and peoples bow down to you. Be lord over your brothers, and may the sons of your mother bow down to you. May those who curse you be cursed and those who bless you be blessed.*

These were not just meaningless words. Isaac had the supernatural faith to believe that God would grant Jacob his blessing. Isaac believed that God would pass on the blessing to his son as well as the future generations.

3 May God Almighty bless you and make you fruitful and increase your numbers until you become a community of peoples (28:3-4).

Jacob hung on to the blessing of his father. When he was about to meet Esau for the first time in many years he cried out, "*9 . . ."O God of my father Abraham, God of my father Isaac, O LORD, who said to me, 'Go back to your country and your relatives, and I will make you prosper,'34*

It was the gift of faith that made Jacob cling to his blessing. Finally, he wrestled with the angel of God until he received his fulfilment. The angel of the Lord not only granted the blessing, but gave Jacob a new name that reflected the prosperity of the Kingdom of God in his life.[35]

---

34   *Genesis 32:9 (NIV)*
35   Genesis 32.224-28

Genesis 28.4

⁴ May he give you and your descendants the blessing given to Abraham, so that you may take possession of the land where you now live as an alien, the land God gave to Abraham."

Blessing over our children

Marilyn and I have two sets of children together. Those wonderful children we gave birth to and then the precious ones we adopted from China. When our first group was growing up, I would go into their rooms before they slept and would speak a blessing over each one of them. Each one had a very specific blessing. We have also prayed for our children's future spouses. If I would miss praying their blessing, they refused to go to sleep until I did. Today, each one of them and their children are dedicated to the Lord and His service. The blessings that were prayed over them have been mostly fulfilled.[36]

Our oldest daughter is married to an Air Force Chaplain; our second daughter married a Christian who is a corporate executive. Both women and their husbands have dynamically affected people around them with the love of Christ. Finally, our son is a worship pastor, is married to a wonderful

---

[36]   They are still living out their lives, so the prophetic word over them is not yet complete.

Christian woman and their children are being raised to love the Lord. Currently, we have three girls from China. The Lord told us before we were married that we would adopt Asian children. We have had visions for each of them and pray that those things will come to pass. We have faith that God will make those things happen.

Elijah the Tishbite – stopping the rain

The Hebrew King Ahab was to bring God's Kingdom to the people. Instead, Ahab married Jezebel who worshipped Baal and Aserah. God was so angered that he brought judgment against Ahab and his kingdom. As judgment, God was going to stop the rain for several years. He gave Elijah power to command the rain to stop and to command it to resume. God supplied the gift of faith to Elijah. It was the supernatural ability to trust God, no matter the circumstances. *Now Elijah the Tishbite, from Tishbe in Gilead, said to Ahab, "As the LORD, the God of Israel, lives, whom I serve, there will be neither dew nor rain in the next few years except at my word (1 Kings 17:1-6)."* Following the pronouncement of the Lord, Elijah was told to hide in the Ravine of Kerith (Place of cutting). Until he moved to another place, God provided for his needs.[37]

---

[37] 1 kings 17.1-6

The gift of faith and raising Lazarus from the dead

After he had said this, he went on to tell them, *"Our friend Lazarus has fallen asleep; but I am going there to wake him up" (John 11:11 (NIV)*

Just like us, Jesus operated in the gifts of the Holy Spirit. While among us, he had to be totally human. Both Mary and Martha approached Jesus and asked why He didn't come when they first let him know that Lazarus was sick. Jesus asked that the stone be rolled away, he said a quick prayer. In it he dialogues with God and thanks God for hearing his request. He then shouts out to Lazarus, ""Lazarus, come out!" (John 11:41-42). God was part of this experience, he provided Jesus with the gift of faith to believe that God would do exactly what he had promised.

Casting out demons

When Jesus stepped ashore in the region of the Gerasenes he was met by a demon possessed man (Luke 8:26 (NIV). The demons in the man said to Jesus, *"What do you want with me, Jesus, Son of the Most High God? I beg you, don't torture me!"*[38]

---

[38] Luke 8.28

Jesus drove the demon out of the man and the man became normal.

Group work:

Study Acts 10:44-48

1. How do you see the gift of faith operating in Peter?

2. How do you think that the gift might work in you?

3. Share your stories with the group.

Group work: Jesus and the storm

Matthew 8:23-27

1. How do we see the gift of faith active in Jesus?

2. Jesus experienced and lived all of the gifts, but what was he really saying to his disciples when he said that they had "little faith?" I think that it was another way for Jesus to say, "Don't you get it?"

3. What kind of reassurance does this give you?

4. The gift of faith can be for a short time to complete a single task, or it can be for a life-time, how have you experienced it?

5. Name at least three Old Testament figures and two New Testament figures that lived a life of faith, you might check the book of Hebrews.

Discussion:

Review 1 Kings 17.

1.   How did Elisha respond to God's direction? How does this reflect the gift of faith?

2.   When God gives direction, do you think that He will also provide the gift of faith to accomplish the task?

REVIEW:

The gift of faith, receives a miracle, and is in operation for prophetic pronouncement, operates when trusting God for provision during famine times. This gift is evident when raising people from the dead, casting demons out of people and when ministering prophetically to others.

This is not a natural gift, it cannot be worked up, but instead accompanies God's miraculous promises to move supernaturally when the situation demands God's remedy.

Challenge:

1. Pray that God will use this gift through you.

2. Ask the Holy Spirit to show you which assignments you can have supernatural faith for.

Gift of Working of Miracles   *Chapter 6*

Definition:

The gift of working of miracles is an intervention in the ordinary operation of nature, a suspension of the rules of nature, a suspension of natural laws. Creating something ex-nihilo.[39]

Intervention in Nature

Elijah and Elisha were walking side by side, when suddenly a chariot of fire and horses of fire appeared. The horses separated Elisha and Elijah from one another. Elijah climbed into the Chariot and went into heaven in something that looked like a whirlwind. Elijah's cloak fell to the ground and Elisha picked it up. He went back to the river Jordan, stood on the bank and struck the water with it. The water divided right from the left and Elisha crossed over to the other side (*2 Kings 2:11-14)*. This miracle proved to the other prophets that Elisha walked in the same "anointing" as Elijah.

Elisha heals the non-potable water of Jericho

---

[39] To create something out of nothing, God forming the earth out of nothing (Genesis 1-2)

In this particular case, Elisha asked for specific things, a bowl filled with salt. He then went to the spring and threw the salt into the spring. Then Elisha announces, 'I have healed this water. From now on it won't cause death. And it won't keep the land from growing crops.' [22] The water was healed. It is still good today (2.19-22). It is obvious from this text that Elisha spoke with God and then followed His directions. This was a gift of faith operating along with the working of miracles to heal the water.

As a young man, Jeremy received Christ in our church and was delivered from severe drug addiction. Several years after his conversion he and several other youth joined with a mission in central Africa. Jeremy loved sharing the Gospel with others, and would take every opportunity to do so. One afternoon, Jeremy and a team of youth were ministering in an African village. Jeremy, excitedly said, "Jesus is so powerful, he can restore sight to the blind." So the villagers went and got a blind person. Jeremy said, "I tried every prayer I could think of, including praying in the name of Jesus." "Nothing worked and I was beginning to panic when a thought hit me, if Jesus spit in the dirt so can I." His mouth was dry and it took a while to work up enough saliva to make mud. He then wiped it on the villager's face and when the mud was washed off, the blind man could see!"**40**

---

[40] Jeremy was a member of "Desert Chapel" in Tucson, Arizona

One can only image how far the story of the healed blind man travelled. The Kingdom certainly came; people understood the power of God.

Jesus changing water into wine

Following Jesus' discussion with his mother, he says to the servants, "Fill the jars with water. . . draw some out and take it to the master of the wedding feast (John 2:1-9). There are several points when the water could have become wine. The first was when the servants poured water into the jars, secondly, when the servants drew a sample, and the third possibility was when the water was being carried to the master. What is important is that Jesus turned the water into wine. This miracle began the supernatural side of Jesus' ministry. Jesus made it clear that he could only do what he saw his father doing.[41] That being the case, Jesus would turn to the Father for directions. This should set a standard for us as we pray for miracles. God, in this case, are there any steps that you want us to take?

"Is there any among us sick?"

While studying to be a pastor in our Lutheran seminary, I struggled with the cessationist position. I did not come from a religious background and just assumed that if the Bible said

---

[41] John 5.19

that we should be praying for the sick, then they should recover. I did discover in short order that this was not what was taught in our Seminary. On the one hand I was taught that all the miracles of the Bible were fact but they had ceased with the formulation of the Canon (Scripture as we have it today). It was also pretty common to have our professors make fun of the Pentecostal churches, especially when it came to speaking in tongues. The challenge I had was when I read Corinthians, Acts, Romans and Ephesians in their original languages, I could not draw the same conclusion. These men were basically following the traditional line. I could not justify the two positions, and did not want to perpetuate the same uncertainty, so instead of going into the ministry, I went into business. To be truthful, I put God on the back shelf for a while.

One morning I was sitting in my business office and I began to pray. "God, if you are real and a God of today, I need to see proof of that." I kept a Bible in my office, I picked it up and it opened to the book of James.[42]

James 5.14-15

"Is any among you sick ...?" He should call the elders of the church to pray over him and anoint him with oil in the name of

---

[42] James 5.13-16 – not a sure fire way to get God's direction

the Lord. [15] *And the prayer offered in faith will make the sick person well; the Lord will raise him up*

If you really are God

After reading this text, I said, "If you are really the God you say you are in the Bible, I will believe in you, and in the Bible if I see a miraculous healing!" When I got home that evening one of our friends dropped by and said, "Bob has been diagnosed with terminal cancer and we want you to pray for him." I immediately called some friends; we anointed Bob with oil and prayed for a miracle. Bob was scheduled to go into the hospital for pre-op and then surgery the next morning. Bob's larynx was riddled with cancer and that was just the tip of the problem. There were no lightning flashes; no one was "slain" in the spirit. We laid hands on Bob, prayed and then sang some songs and he went home.

Late the next morning I received a call from Bob. There has been no surgery. On their initial exam the doctors could find no cancer. Bob was in a teaching hospital so there was a variety of experience among the members of the surgical team. The head surgeon had asked one of the interns to scope Bob's throat and describe what he saw. The intern said that all he saw was a perfectly normal throat and larynx. The surgeon said a few choice words, grabbed the scope and looked for himself. There was no visible cancer. The surgeon had seen Bob the day before and had told him that he had terminal cancer. Now that there was no visible cancer twenty-four hours later the doctor said to Bob, "Did you take any new medication?" Bob said, "Yes, good old doctor Jesus." After one hundred and twenty needle biopsies Bob was declared to be cancer free. There was a double miracle, Bob was healed and I dedicated my life to Christ. Despite what I had been taught in Seminary, God was still in the miracle business.

Working of miracles for deliverance

In preparation for the deliverance of the Children of Israel from Egypt, God appeared to Moses and revealed His divine name for the first time.[43] God then gave Moses and Aaron specific instructions for the deliverance of the Children of Israel.

When Moses dealt with Pharaoh, miracles took place to show that God's power was greater than Pharaoh and the gods of Egypt (Exodus 7-14). Every Egyptian god was overcome through a miraculous plague, including the first born of pharaoh. For the children of Israel to be totally free from Egypt they had to see that God would overcome everything that would prevent their freedom to worship Him.

---

[43] **Exodus 3.14** - יהוה *hawyah* I AM THAT I AM or I AM THE EVER BECOMING ONE

Provision for Elijah and the widow

When the water dried up in the brook of Cherith[44] God commanded Elijah to move to Zarephath[45] and there a widow would supply him with food. When he arrived there was a widow gathering wood to prepare her last meal. Elijah asked her to bring him water to drink and a piece of bread. Considering that this was a time of draught and famine that would be a lot to ask. Elijah instructed her, *"Don't be afraid. Go home and do as you have said. But first make a small cake of bread for me from what you have and bring it to me, and then make something for yourself and your son (1 Kings 17.12).*

Elijah conveyed his faith in God's by saying to the widow, if you make a cake for Elijah, God would replenish the flour and oil every day for Elijah and there will be more than enough for you and your family until the Lord causes it to rain (17.14). We learn from Elijah's example that miracles can be a direct product of our obedience to him. Both Elijah and the woman underwent a refining process. They learned to trust God despite the circumstances. The woman learned that God would provide for her family if she trusted the word of God's prophet.

---

44 כְּרִית kerît – root: to cut

45 דְּבַר Dawbar Place of refinement

Group Discussion:

1. In the story of Elijah and the widow discuss how you see the gift of faith working alongside the working of Miracles.
2. As a group, work on a definition of the working of miracles that is easily understood.

Opening of the Red Sea

Read about the parting of the Red Sea.

1. How many miracles is there (Exodus 14.21-31)?

2. How many gifts of the Holy Spirit do you see in action?

Feeding of the five-thousand John 6:5-14

Group discussion

1. What gifts do you see in operation?
2. What process did Jesus use to build faith in his disciples?

3. How did Jesus show that something special was about to happen? How did people respond after the miracle?

5. Discuss the types of situations where these gifts may be encouraged

6. Prepare to go on treasure hunts, ask the Lord to identify the people you need to minister to.

Read Acts13-4.12

Paul announces blindness upon the sorcerer Bar Jesus.[46]

This action was a sign to everyone; it showed that God is all powerful and that His word has authority and power.

1. List three examples from the Old and New Testament where the working of miracles can be identified.

2. As a group, identify how God will use this gift through each of you.

---

[46] Elymas the sorcerers name in Greek.

Gifts of Healing   Chapter 7

Definition: As the name suggests, there are many healings that fall under this label. It is generally understood to heal the condition, but the body uses its own God given resources to return to full strength. I think it very important for the Body of Christ to seek out who has the gifts for specific maladies. It seems to me that when a person has a specific disease, it only is natural to seek out the people that operate in those specific gifts of healing. For instance, if someone consistently sees healing of breast cancer, then maybe when people get that disease they should be prayed for by the person with that specific gift. It certainly would be an encouragement for the body of Christ to work together.

If a person with lung cancer is prayed for and they are healed. The body is still wasted away. It will take time for the body to regenerate itself.   The disease is healed at its root, now the effects of the disease have to be restored.

Kenneth Hagen's grandson – And medical science

Kenneth Hagin's grandson had been prayed over for an inoperable brain tumor many times. God did not move through gifts of healing or working of miracles.[47]   Kenneth Hagin

---

[47] Story told by Oral Roberts at an Oral Roberts conference which I attended. City of Faith was a Christian hospital on the Oral Roberts

called Oral Roberts asking for help. Craig Hagin, Kenneth's grandson, had what doctors had called an inoperable brain tumor. Craig was checked in at City of Faith Hospital and put in the hands of spirit filled neurosurgeon. The Cat-Scan showed that if the pressure could not be relieved, the little boy would pass away quickly. The surgeon stayed up all night seeking a way to remove the tumour that had been termed inoperable. Just as dawn was approaching, the surgeon had a vision and in it he was shown the steps to safely remove the tumour. Craig is alive and has a family today.

Kenneth Hagin

I believe in natural healing and I thank God for it. I think one of the greatest areas in medical science, and one in which the greatest strides have been made, is in the field of preventive medicine. But not only do I believe in natural healing, I also believe in supernatural healing.[48]

Heal the sick!

When Jesus sent his disciples out to the Jews He gave them authority to cast out evil spirits and to heal a variety of diseases.[49] At the same time, the disciples were to announce that the Kingdom of Heaven was near. The command was a mixture of the gifts of healing and the working of miracles and

---

Campus.

[48] Story told by Kenneth Hagin at Oral Roberts conference which I attended.

[49] Matthew 10.1-8

the gift of faith. The disciples giving these gifts away freely brought the Kingdom of Heaven near. These acts made it easy for people to "experience" God.

Same principles hold true today

Our youth pastors, Paul and Tricia Short here at Connections AVC, started a group called the "Unseen[50]." They travel from church to church and teach the young people how to minister in the gifts of the Spirit.[51] One of the things that *The Unseen* group teach is "treasure hunting.*"[52]* This encourages the seeking of direction from the Holy Spirit as a group. Each person in the group asks of God, "How can I identify the person you want me to pray for?" They also ask, "Is there anyone that you want to heal? What do you want us to do?" They then travel to a mall, park, beach or someplace that the Lord directs and begin to look for the people that God identified. No one is surprised when the Holy Spirit ministers to perfect strangers. The young ministers come back with their faith bolstered with many exciting stories. They see a variety of healings ranging from emotional, relational all the way to physical.

---

[50] The ever growing Techno oriented young people who have little or no face to face social contact; they are "Unseen."

[51] *Unseen* launched by Pastors Paul and Tricia Short to teach the "unseen" generations how to minister in the power of the Spirit.

[52] The youth ask God who they should minister to in Malls, large stores and parks. They might get "red sweater" or bald head. They then look for those people.

Mark 9:17-29

One of the men in the crowd spoke up and said, "Teacher, I brought my son for you to heal him. He can't speak because he is possessed by an evil spirit that won't let him talk. [18] And whenever this evil spirit seizes him, it throws him violently to the ground and makes him foam at the mouth and grind his teeth and become rigid. So I asked your disciples to cast out the evil spirit, but they couldn't do it."

When Jesus sent his disciples out, they got to do what they saw Jesus doing. This was a training time for the disciples. In less than three years they had to be equipped to do the very things that Jesus had.[53] Can you imagine how the disciples must have felt when the boy's father said, "So I asked your disciples to cast out the evil spirit, but they couldn't do it? "The disciples had been sent out in the power and authority of Jesus to heal the sick and to cast out demons. They did not always know what to do. In the case of the boy who was controlled by demons they did their best, but there was one thing that they left out. They should have asked God what to do.[54]

What are your instructions?

---

[53] John 14.12

[54] The disciples did not know how to deal with a demon possessed boy.

There are many times while ministering that we run into things that stump us. Those are the times when we should go to God and say, "God, I do not know what to do! What are your instructions?"[55] The reason Jesus said, "This kind can only come out through prayer and fasting" was to point out the disciple's need to ask God for instructions before proceeding. So often we get stumped with how we should pray that we forget that God already has the answer.

Cancer - dead or alive

The day before travelling to China for our second adoption trip I had a number of needle biopsies to check for prostate cancer. This is the leading killer cancers of men. The digital exam didn't show anything out of the ordinary. In fact, the doctor had typed on the screen "no cancer visible." So off to China I went to adopt our second daughter. The day we returned to Tucson, there was a message on the phone, "Rick and Marilyn, I want to see you in my office as soon as possible." A few days later I had radical cancer surgery.

Not a very good patient

I truly don't make a very good patient. Because of that, Marilyn reminded me, "Rick, you are a pastor and your behaviour has to be exceptional. The night of my surgery I

---

[55] Mark 9.29

was teamed with another cancer patient who knew how to put down the nurses, and it seemed that he also had full usage of every swear word invented. Just as he would cut down, I would call the nurse over and give them praise.

About two in the morning my roommate was going strong, but he had started swearing using God's name. I called the head nurse and asked if they could find me a different room. The nurses said to me, you have treated us so well; we are going to give you a room of your own.

You have hurt your back!

There I lay with what seemed like tons of tubes going in and out of my body. On the second night the late shift nurse came in and the Lord showed me that she had seriously injured her back. She was in a great deal of pain and was afraid of losing her job because of it. It was hard for her to lift and shift patients. I said to her, "You have hurt your back and are in a lot of pain." She grabbed her back and then said, "Do you mean it shows that bad?" I said, "No, it doesn't show at all." "The Lord showed me that you had injured your back." I said to her, "Come over here and I will pray for you." She very hesitantly took my hands and I asked God to heal her back. It was that simple.

The next evening she came dancing into my room saying, "God healed me!" The word was out among the medical staff in the cancer ward. The staff was extraordinarily kind and helpful for the remainder of my stay. The day I was to check out, a head nurse came into my room, knelt on the hospital floor and began to pray for my family and me. I had never met her before or talked with her since. It was shortly thereafter that I was told that I was cancer free. I believe that it was the combined efforts of the surgeon (who also prayed) and the head nurse that insured that I would be cancer free.

Group work:

Read Mark 9.14-19

1.   Discuss God's goodness and his love of mankind.

2. Did the Spirit of God move perfectly in Jesus? How so?

3. Was Jesus truly in tune with the Word, the Father and the Spirit?

4. Is it possible for us to have that same sensitivity?

5. What exactly did Jesus mean when he said: *"Anything is possible if a person believes?"*

6. Is this an extraordinary burden if we are not healed supernaturally?

7. Some turn a lack of healing into blame on others; then it becomes a burden.

8. Explain healing or the lack of it in Kingdom terms

9. What was the best that father could offer?

    How about the disciples?

10. What was Jesus' response? This puzzled the disciples.

11. The disciples were men of faith and action.

12. How did Jesus respond to His disciples?

13. What have you learned from this story about healings and miracles?

Lessons about ministry

1. Go in the name of Jesus, that is, go with His authority.

2. Respond to the needs of others.

3.   Pray with expectation, knowing the miracle or healing is up to God.

4.   If the person is not healed, then ask God if there is anything more that you can do.

5.   Remember - there are no magic formulas

No Magic Formulas

During the end of service ministry time a visitor had worked her way into a prayer team. She immediately began spewing formulas at the person seeking help; it was obvious that she did not have a clue about God's care and love for people. She was back in service the following week, so I said, "In a few minutes we are going to have ministry time. In the Vineyard we do not use formula prayers. For instance, we do not believe that you have to end all prayers in Jesus name or that you have to use King James English." "Let's get out from under all of these bondages. " "If someone has a bad back just say, 'God, Joe has a bad back, please heal it." Then ask the person, "What are you feeling?" The visitor has now become a regular attender and no longer uses formula when praying for people.

Group work:

Jesus tells his disciples that he and his Father (God) are one. Then he draws focus on the supernatural works that he has done. He then makes a very important statement, *"The truth is, anyone who believes in me will do the same works I have done, and even greater works because I am going to the*

Father."[56] He then makes the statement, *"You can ask for anything (works that Jesus did) and I will do it..."[57]*

[15] *"If (since) you love me, obey my commandments. [58]* [16] *And I will ask the Father, and he will give you another Counsellor, who will never leave you.*

1.   What can we ask of the Father when praying for people?

2.   What does it mean to do the same works as Jesus? How many can you find in the book of Luke?

3.   What does love of God have to do with the way people understand God?

Make a list of Jesus' commands: (Matt. 6.5-8.29)

1.   Do not be angry with your brother without cause.

2.   Do not name a brother something that he is not.

The Gift of Prophecy   Chapter 8

Definition: Prophecy is communicating a message from God to his people. It is not to be confused with the prophetic ministry or function.[59] Prophecy could be about events in the present or future in the lives of people or actual events in the

---

[56] John 14.10-12

[57] 14.13

[58] 'Ἐάν - eh-an' - Can be translated If or since. I.e. "Since you love me" seems to fit the context better in this instance

[59] 1 Corinthians 12.10

present or future. The gift of prophecy is often confused with the prophetic ministry. The truth of the matter is that God uses a variety of people to deliver prophecy. In the generic sense, the gifts of the word of knowledge and wisdom are often thought of as prophetic gifts as well.

Misuse of Prophecy

We have all seen the prophetic gift misused. Sometimes, as pastors, we would rather not have to deal with people who have a strange concept of the role of the Old Testament prophet. They think that since Elijah and other prophets of the Old Testament corrected the Kings and nations then that is the role that they should be playing today. They fail to see that in the Old Testament, the Jewish Kings were a type for King Jesus so their lives had to reflect God. When that did not happen, then the Old Testament Prophets were charged to bring the kings to righteousness. A classic example is the relationship between Samuel and Saul. [60]

Dr. Wayne Grudem says of prophecy: "In conclusion, there is a danger that prophecy will be over-valued, and there is the opposite danger that it will be rejected altogether. To avoid both of those common errors, we should understand the authority of prophecy correctly, as something that a God can use to bring things to our attention, but as something that nonetheless can contain human interpretation and mistakes. It

[60] 1 Samuel 13.13-14

must therefore be subject to Scripture and must be regulated and tested according to Paul's instructions in 1 Corinthians 14. In brief for, therefore, a modern application of this chapter would be just what Paul told the Thessalonians: *"Do not quench the Spirit, do not despise prophesying, but test everything; hold fast what is good."* (1 Thessalonians 5:19-21, RSV)[61]

Components of modern day prophecy

With the establishment of Christ's kingdom, there is no need for the supposed Old Testament model. Prophecy, then, takes on a whole new look. According to Paul in his letter to the Corinthians, prophecy is to have three major components. First, prophecy is to help others grow or mature in Christ.[62] Second, prophecy brings direct words of encouragement to the believer.[63] It can also mean to stand alongside a person in their trial. Jesus promised that when He went away, he would send another, the Holy Spirit, the paraklētos.[64] The words that the Holy Spirit speaks through us will bring to us the elements that we see in the Holy Spirit Himself. Finally, the prophetic is to bring comfort.[65] It should be noted that each

---

[61] *The Gift of Prophecy in New Testament times and Today*- Dr. Wayne Grudem – *pp. 93-94* – Crossway Books- 2000-ISBN 978-58134-243-713:

[62] *Οἰκοδομή* - oikodomē – To build up or to edify.

[63] *παράκλησις* – paraklēsis - Comfort, Comforter, Consolation, Console, Encourage, Entreat.

[64] *Παράκλητος*- paraklētos- Holy Spirit, comforter, counselor, encourager.

of these requirements come directly from the person and nature of the Holy Spirit himself. Those who bring prophecy need to remember that prophecy today brings life to the receiver.[66]

"God hates your worship"

In one of our church plants, we had attracted quite a number of unschooled "prophets." If we conducted our services differently than they were used to, they would use "prophecy" to attempt to "guide" us back. Our service style was contemporary Charismatic. This seemed to be difficult for "some old time Pentecostals." One area particularly that was frowned upon was our contemporary worship. We had a new worship leader who was quite good at leading people to a place of celebrating God; our style was contemporary which most people in our congregation enjoyed. We had one Pentecostal woman who declared to all that she was a "Pentecostal prophetess" and she didn't care for our worship at all.[67] One Sunday after a very spirit filled time of worship; she stood up and said, "Verily, verily thus saith the Lord, 'I hate your worship!!" I stood and corrected her in front of the congregation, but I also charged her by saying, "you no longer have permission to bring what you think is prophecy before

---

[65] $\pi\alpha\rho\alpha\mu\upsilon\theta\iota\alpha$ – paramythia – Comfort, comforter, to console, consolation.

[66] 1 Corinthians 14.3, Exhort

[67]Some Pentecostal prophets seemed to be unschooled in the roll of the NT prophet.

this congregation." I also explained the elements of prophecy to the entire congregation. I warned the lady that if she did anything like this again, I would ask her to leave the church. In her view this became a battle of wills; that of a prophetess who is never wrong, and a pastor who has sold out to the Devil.[68]

A lesson yet to be learned

The following Sunday she stood and began, "Verily, verily …" That was all I allowed her to say. That evening I went to their home and said, "It is obvious that you will not accept guidance from me as your pastor. Remember I told you last week if you tried this again, you would be asked to leave. Since you attempted to do this again I can see that you are very divisive and you may not return." While it was not comfortable to do, it was essential to stop this kind of "prophecy" before it took root. This woman could not tell the difference between her own personal agenda and the word of God if held against the guidelines that Paul gives for this gift[69]

Anyone can bring prophecy

[68] I was the pastor and very dedicated to the Lord.

[69] Spiritual growth, encouragement and comfort.

As is the case for all prophecy today, it must be measured against the nature and character of Christ as well as the three components that Paul mentions in his letter to the Corinthians.[70] Peter said in his Pentecost sermon, *"[17] "'In the last days, God says, I will pour out my Spirit on all people. Your sons and daughters will prophesy, your young men will see visions, your old men will dream dreams. [18] Even on my servants, both men and women, I will pour out my Spirit in those days, and they will prophesy (Acts 2:17-18).*

Anyone can bring prophesy. It is not a special badge of acceptance by the Holy Spirit. I think that this gift should be sought after in small groups, large groups, church services and in as many venues that we think that God wants to make Himself known. A good learning place should be in small groups though.

Small group miracle

Several years ago, a new couple to the church joined our small group.

Our standard for small groups is to make new people the focus of the prophetic. My instructions are usually, "Let's get quiet before the Lord. Some of you will get a scripture, others a vision and some of you will hear God speaking. Doug called

---

[70] 1 Corinthians 14.2

himself bubble boy because he was afraid to come out of his shell. Often he would say, "My antennae are not working, all I get is static." This went on for a few months but the Holy Spirit had me change direction. I said, "All of you can hear God speak, you just don't know how to explain what you are seeing. Either that or you are afraid of being wrong. So this time, during the week, I want you to write down what God shows you. This was all Doug needed. In his words, "I have come out of my bubble." Doug is frequently seen bringing a word from the Lord to people. Finally, Doug holds the record for being down and out under the power of the Spirit. We had a fire tunnel[71] Doug just started down the tunnel and just dropped down on the floor. He was out for around five hours.

God speaks to adoptive parents with children from China

I had been conversing with adoptive parents from China who wanted to adopt children from China. At that time China was being overwhelmed with applications for adoption and their administrative abilities were overtaxed. When Marilyn and I started our process there were around 250 adoptive parents. Two and one half years later there were over three thousand applications from America. Because of this huge number of applications in such a short time the whole process came to a standstill. Future adoptive parents were very discouraged and

---

[71] People line up in a double row facing each other like a tunnel. They then pray for those who walk through the tunnel. Because the Holy Spirit is in the midst of the tunnel, it is called a "fire tunnel."

many were encouraged to switch countries. This meant that parents would have years to wait before their applications would even be looked at.

It was my normal practice to start praying about 2:00 am and then finish at 6.00am. I did this for two and one half years.

Vision of an ornate Chinese gateway

One morning as I prayed, I saw a vision of a very ornate closed gate[72] and behind it was children backed up for as far as I could see. Then I saw the gate open and children began racing through. I immediately went on the internet, shared my vision, and notified the waiting families (about 3,000) that the gateways of China were now open to release the children from China. I also felt that it was important to say that this was happening now and people would be notified by the end of the week. I also said, "Do not switch to a new country, but stay with China."

That morning a couple came into my office and said, "We cannot face any more disappointment, we are going to withdraw from adoption altogether." I shared with them the vision that I had that morning and encouraged them to give it a

---

[72] Gates are very important in China. All towns and villages have gates many are very ornately decorated. In small towns it is the custom to have the village Chief meet you at the gate and invite you in personally.

little more time.[73] That couple now has two daughters from China.

Seeing into the future

Potential adoptive parents asked a number of questions about how I knew that adoptions would resume. I openly shared my relationship with Christ and talked about God being active in our lives today. One person in particular wrote me from back East and said, "What kind of pastor are you, if you can see into the future?" She was not familiar with Charismatics and so I explained how God loved us and wanted to work through us as He did me. In the end she moved to Tucson and was married. Sherrie and her husband Steve attended one of our small groups that I was leading. As we prayed for them we saw them with several Chinese children, but we also saw them operating as missionaries in China.

When their first referral arrived, Sherrie stated that she couldn't go because she had a phobia of flying. [74] As the group prayed for her, a prophetic word came telling her to trust in the Lord and she would not only go the first time, but

---

[73] They have since adopted two daughters

[74] Referral: After producing mountains of paperwork requesting a Chinese child that had been abandoned, the Chinese Adoption Agency in Beijing send adoptive parents a photo and medical information on a child. The parent could accept or reject. We always took the first one because we believed that God was in total control of the child's selection.

would go to China many times. Sherrie and Steve now have four Chinese daughters.

About two years before our adoption of our first daughter, I began to see visions of our daughter. Later, I was sitting in my office and I heard a young child crying hysterically. I went to my office manager and said, "Would you please go check on that child?" Marlys looked at me with a look that said, "Here we go again." There was no child, but it was the day that our daughter was taken from her foster family and put in the orphanage.

There was the child that I had seen!

When we arrived in China, the children were brought in for us to pick up. There were over twenty children in the room. I walked over to the child that I had seen for those last two years. Through dreams and visions God showed me very vividly our daughter.

Agabus and the severe famine

Agabus brought a prophecy warning of a sever famine throughout the Roman world. The Christian leaders collected money and food to provide for the Christians in Judea (Acts 11.28)

Agabus visited Paul while he was staying with Philip the Evangelist.[75] Agabus took Paul's belt and tied up his own feet and hands and prophesied that if Paul traveled to Jerusalem, the Jewish leaders would tie him up and turned over to the Romans. Paul's disciples were upset, but Paul rejoiced because he knew that he would be taken before the Roman Emperor. The final stages of his ministry would take place in Rome. Agabus encouraged Paul by confirming what was about to happen in his life. It is obvious that Paul already had this information from God.

Don't stifle the Holy Spirit

In Paul's first letter to the Thessalonians, guidelines are given for healthy relationships with one another and with the Holy Spirit.[76] Paul said, *Warn the lazy, encourage the timid and care for the weak.* Don't imitate evil in your actions, be filled with the joy of the Lord, and keep on keeping on in prayer. More than likely Paul is addressing Roman soldiers who have dedicated their lives to Christ. He is essentially saying, "Christians must be different." Despite the situations that are faced always be full of joy. Then Paul makes two very important statements: *[19] Do not stifle the Holy Spirit.[20] Do not scoff at prophecies, [21] but test everything that is said. Hold on to what is good.*

---

[75] Acts 21.8-14

[76] 1 Thessalonians 5.14-21

Rev. Harald Bredesen

Reverend Harald Bredesen had many friends, and I am very blessed to have been one of them. He was particularly good at hearing God's voice for future events. [77] But he was also good at reading people's mail. He was certainly a Charismatic giant of our faith. I asked him, "Harald, when God tells you to go somewhere how do you measure if it is God speaking or just a desire of yours?" He said, "That is easy. God always gives me the impossible to do." He said, "Rick, make it easy on yourself and hard for God." "For example, I was just finishing up a speaking tour and was in the Orly airport in Paris, France. I was out of money and had my final ticket home. I heard the Lord speaking to me that I was to travel throughout the Soviet Union."[78] He said, "Rick, this is what I said, 'God, my flight boards in twenty minutes. If you want me to go to the Soviet Union, then you have ten minutes to call me over the airport public address system. I will be given tickets and money for all of my travelling expenses." Harald, then, just sat back and relaxed. Before the ten minutes were up, Harald had been called over the airport public communication booth and there was a packet with his itinerary, money and airline tickets. I can't say that I have walked the same way as Harald, but he had a huge impact on my life.

---

[77] Rev. Harald Bredesen was a Lutheran and considered to be one of the giants of the Charismatic movements. He is also the author of Yes, Lord, Gospel Light 2008 ISBN: 0830745351

[78] This was years before the Berlin wall came down.

Misconceptions of prophecy

When it comes to prophecy, there are many misconceptions. One of them is that if your prophecy doesn't come true, then you should be stoned. While I haven't heard that one in a while, there are many others whose purpose is shut people down in fear. The only way to move in the prophetic is to step out and say what you think God is saying. A good place to begin is in small groups, but with people who have a real desire to move in the gifts of the Spirit. As you gain confidence, you may speak in larger meetings and eventually in a church service.

Scholars see prophecy through the life and Ministry of Jesus

There is an abundance of evidence to show that Jesus was popularly regarded as a great prophet and that he himself accepted this designation (of prophet). The passages which have been quoted do not bear out the contention of

R. Bultman that Jesus was characterised as a prophet on the basis of the eschatological purpose alone. It was rather the whole impression of his purpose, work and person which gave him the right to this title.[79]

---

[79] *Prophecy in Early Christianity and the Ancient Mediterranean World*, David E. Aune, p. 3-Wlliam B Eerdmans Publishing Company- ISBN 0-

How to get started

One of best ways to get started is in a small group. If I have a new group that I am trying to train, I will pick one person (Let's call this person Bill) in the group that everyone will minister to. Then I have everyone get quiet and I say, "You may have a vision, an inner voice, a clear voice, an impression or a specific Bible passage that the Lord brings to mind." Share what you see as soon as you get it. I then encourage the others to listen to the Holy Spirit while each person shares.

Beer Steins and Stuffed Animals

One evening our small group was packed out. That night we had two guests that we were ministering to. They were husband/wife team and both were Tucson police officers. Following our Bible Studies, we then turned to ministry. Before we moved into penetrating ministry, the Holy Spirit let the couple know that he knew what was in their hearts.

One of the men said, "I am not sure that this will mean anything, but I see a whole bunch of mugs." Dave who brought the word was a conservative Christian so he didn't want to talk about beer. I said, "Dave you didn't see mugs, you saw beer steins." The husband police officer said, "Wow! I collect beer steins from all over the world." One of our ladies said, "I see a lot of stuffed teddy bears." The wife police officer said, "I collect stuffed animals." These "words of knowledge" made it possible for the couple to receive the prophecies that were given that night.

Group work:

1. Pick a person from your group to minister to.

2. Get quiet before the Lord and ask Him to reveal information about the person you are ministering to.

3. The leader of the group should coach the others. For example, "Is anyone getting anything? Are you having visions?"

Different Kinds of Tongues   Chapter 9

What was the church in Corinth like? While they operated in the gifts of the spirit, they lived like the pagans. They were overly confident in their "gifts" and therefore better than others. They believed that they were superior if they spoke in tongues because that was the "language of angels." It was almost as if they competed back and forth with tongues. They certainly did not care much for the poor in their presence. It is within this setting that Paul discusses how the gifts should be used in the service. In the Vineyard we have churches of all sizes. The gifts are less likely to be used in the larger church services, but they are encouraged in the small groups. The Corinthians thought that because they were speaking in the "language of angels" they were better than Paul or any other person who is not part of their clique.[80]

---

[80] Gordon D. Fee – *God's Empowering Presence, The Holy Spirit in the Letters of Paul* – Hendrickson, publisher, 1994 –page 89-ISBN:

Tongues as a dialect of another person

There are a number of ways that tongues manifests. It can be in the dialect of another person. This happened on Pentecost day. Those in the upper room began to speak in the dialects of those who came to see what was causing such a stir.

[4] And they were all filled with the Holy Ghost, and began to speak with   other tongues, as the Spirit gave them utterance. [5] And there were dwelling at Jerusalem Jews, devout men, out of every nation under heaven
[6] Now when this was noised abroad, the multitude came together, and were confounded, because that every man heard them speak in his own language (2:4-6).

Tongues for personal edification

[4] He who speaks in a tongue edifies himself, but he who prophesies edifies the church (1 Corinthians 14:4).

Each person speaking in tongues outside of the service will be edified by God himself. There is no great mystery here. Speaking in tongues edifies or builds up the individual. Speaking prophetically edifies the church.   Paul is not denigrating tongues at all.   Paul is saying that speaking in tongues to communicate directly with God builds up the individual spiritually.   Having been built up, then the gift of

094357594X

prophecy is brought into the church for its edification. The more we get, the more we give away in the context of the church service.

In the late sixties the gifts of the Holy Spirit were quite exciting to watch and to participate in. My Lutheran pastor gave me a book entitled, *They Speak with Other Tongues.*[81] Because my specialty was doctrine or teaching of the church, he asked me to read this book to see if it was *scriptural.* My wife, Marilyn and I both consumed the book and began praying for that experience for ourselves. How we got it is another story.

Harald Bredesen – Mr. Charismatic

One of the stories in the book is about Harald Bredesen. Harald was a Pastor who would later become our friend.

As Harald told the story, he was at a Nobel Peace Prize convention. He was in casual conversation with a friend, when the Holy Spirit told him to go over to an Egyptian woman and speak to her in tongues. Harald wrestled with God as he approached the woman. He kept asking God what to say. He casually knew the woman. He said to her, "Have you ever heard this language before?" She was shocked because Harald was speaking in the dialect of this woman's

---

[81] *They Speak with Other Tongues,* John L Sherrill, Chosen Publishing Company, 1991-ISBN: ISBN: 0800791304

home town in Egypt. When asked what Harald had said, she explained that God was telling her to rededicate her life to Christ. To her credit, she did exactly that. This lady was a very important lady politically and socially in Egypt. She opened the door for Harald to pray with Anwar Sadat, King Hussein and Meacham Began just prior to the Middle East Peace Accords. [82] Harald presented Anwar Sadat and The King Hussein of Jordan the *Prince of Peace Award. Sadat called the occasion he received the award "the high point of my entire life, more important to me even than the Nobel Peace Prize. That was in the political arena. This was spiritual."*[83]

Tongues as a sign

Since the Corinthians were misusing speaking in tongues Paul reminds them what the purpose was. It provides a wonderful means of communication between your spirit and God's. Paul says to the Corinthians, "*2 For anyone who speaks in a tongue does not speak to men but to God. Indeed, no one understands him; he utters mysteries with his spirit (1 Corinthians 14:2).* This is hardly a negative to communicate with God. Paul goes on to remind the Corinthians what the purpose of tongues

---

[82] This story was shared with by Harald Bredesen himself. He was frequently referred to as "Mr. Charismatic.

[83] Wikipedia – Article: Harald Bredesen http://en.wikipedia.org/wiki/Harald_Bredesen

is. It is to edify or build up the individual within the context of a service. I also believe that singing in the spirit might fall under the same classification.

So often we get lost in Paul's admonition to focus on prophecy while in the services. When we study this gift we cannot forget that since the Corinthian church had placed such a high priority on speaking in tongues, Paul gave prophecy a position above speaking in tongues.[84]

Receiving the gift of tongues has nothing to do with Christian maturity, nor does it make one person better than another. The language is not learned nor is it understood in the mind of the one speaking it. It is both a gift and miracle for believers to receive. Finally, we speak in tongues because it is one of the gifts promised to us by the Great Commission.

Yelling in tongues

When I was a fairly new pastor, I took over what had been a Four Square church. While I had plenty of experience with the

[84] [5] *I would like every one of you to speak in tongues, but I would rather have you prophesy. He who prophesies is greater than one who speaks in tongues, unless he interprets, so that the church may be edified (1 Corinthians 14:5)*

.

Charismatic Movement, I had next to no experience with Pentecostal Churches. Once I decided to accept the call to this church, they ran a full page advertisement describing my experience and education. As a result, we had a number of professional people come to our service. Everything went well until we had an altar call for the sick. A person came forward for prayer and two Pentecostal women began yelling very loudly in tongues. All of the professional visitors and their families hit the rear doors at a dead run, and I wanted to be with them. "That display did not help anyone," I thought to myself, "now I know what Paul was dealing with!"

Twenty years after Pentecost

Twenty years after Pentecost Paul discovered believers in Ephesus who had not received the Holy Spirit. After a brief explanation, Paul laid hands on them. [5]

As soon as they heard this, they were baptized in the name of the Lord Jesus. [6] Then Paul laid his hands on them, the Holy Spirit came on them, and they spoke in other tongues and prophesied (Acts 19.5-6)

Speaking in tongues is a gift that Paul gives high value to. He claims to speak in tongues more than anyone else in Corinth. Paul continues to draw a contrast between speaking out loud in tongues and singing in tongues. Paul says, *Pray for the understanding or for the interpretation.* [85]

Group Work:

1. Why is it important for Paul to say, "I speak in tongues more   than all of you?

2. List out the benefits of tongues.

3. Spend time alone with God and pray in tongues. Allow yourself to be edified by the Holy Spirit.

4. Break up into small groups of three to four. Pray in tongues and then share what God gives you.

5. Why do you think speaking in tongues is given such prominence in the Great Commission?

6. What gifts of the Spirit does this gift open the doorway to?

7. Why are tongues a sign for the unbeliever outside the church service but not within the church service?

   a. What scriptures would you use to make your point?

8. Begin with Pentecost and document all cases of the outpouring of tongues?

9. Now study 1 Corinthians and the Gospels and document all incidences of tongues

---

[85] 1 Corinthians 14:15

10. Why would Jesus promise speaking in tongues in the Great Commission if it were not important to the Church?

11. List out the number of benefits for speaking in tongues.

Tongues and Interpretation   *Chapter 10*

Paul says in I Corinthians chapter 14, *the gifts used in a service should be in languages people understand. While it is good to speak in tongues, a greater purpose is served if the message is brought forth in prophecy or with tongues and interpretation.* Paul makes it very clear when he says, *"Since you are eager to have spiritual gifts, try to excel in gifts that build up the church* (1 Corinthians 14.12).

Classically, we think that interpretation is only through direct translation. I think that it is far greater than that. The interpretation could come in a vision. Outside the context of the church, dreams could also bring the interpretation of one praying in the spirit. I also believe that tongues are a catalyst when praying for the sick or when preparing "treasure hunts."[86]

---

[86] Seeking God to reveal who a ministry team should minister to we do this in malls or other public places.

Speaking out in tongues is a language to God, but if the language is to be said aloud, then there should be an interpreter. Paul points out that the focus for everyone in a service is to minister to people in ways that they can understand. Paul gives guidance for a variety of ways in which tongues is acceptable for the church service. Paul makes it clear that in the service there are acceptable ways that prophecy and tongues can be utilized to the benefit of all. He admonishes, *"No more than two or three should speak in an unknown language. They must speak one at a time, and someone must be ready to interpret what they are saying (I Corinthians 14:13).*

Paul adds a new dimension to tongues in a service. The Word says that each person who has a message in tongues needs to be silent until they know for sure that an interpreter is present. This means that people who move prophetically and in tongues and interpretation should also be working on accurately hearing God speak. The tongue speaker has freedom to speak out in tongues if they know that there is an interpretation.

He who prophesies is greater than one who speaks in tongues, unless he interprets, so that the church may be edified. I also believe that the person speaking in tongues can interpret their own tongue. Paul adds an entirely new dimension.

He says, *"[15] what is it then? I will pray with the spirit, and I will pray with the understanding also: I will sing with the spirit, and I will sing with the understanding also (I Corinthians 14:15).*

Paul provides a focus that is new to the Corinthians. In the service all operate in their gifts for the benefit of the body. If I seek to pray in the spirit, then I should also seek to interpret the message. If I sing in the spirit, then I should be prepared to interpret.

Oral Roberts

When I was doing graduate studies at Oral Roberts Seminary, Dr. Roberts addressed us on the subject of tongues and interpretation.[87] This simple teaching helped me to understand a number spiritual releases that I experienced. I pray a great deal in tongues and that quite often is followed by visions or dreams. Many times I will get an answer to something that I have sought God for.

Rick, Steve is lost!

In Tucson, we have one huge swap meet that is open during the weekends. Thousands of people attend at the same time. It is easy for kids to get lost. Steve, our eleven year old son

---

[87] I was personally present at the conference and was captivated by the thought of interpreting my own tongue.

went with Marilyn to the swap meet. I stayed at home to do some studying. The phone rang and it was Marilyn and she frantically said, "Rick, Steve is lost!" She had looked all over the swap meet and Steve was not to be found. I said, "Marilyn, hang up and call me back in five minutes and I'll tell you where he is." I then began to pray in tongues. After a few minutes I saw a vision of the swap meet from the air. I could be as close or as far away as I wanted. I saw Steve kneeling behind a book rack reading comic books. Marilyn called back and she said, "What have you seen?" I said, "Where are you?" She replied, "I am right in the middle by a very tall telephone pole with phones attached to it." I could see the pole and I directed Marilyn right to Steve. He had been out of sight because he was on the ground captivated by the comic book that he was reading. I said to Marilyn, "Call me back when you find him." A few minutes later, Marilyn called. She said, "Rick, Steve was exactly where you said he would be."

1 Cor. 14:27-28

28 But if no one is present who can interpret, they must be silent in your church meeting and speak in tongues to God privately.

Paul tells the Corinthian church that no more than three should be speaking out at one time. Other people should be seeking the Lord so that they can bring an interpretation. This is a requirement that the Corinthians learn how to work together so that all are able to participate in ministry.

Group Work:

1. How does the author use tongues and interpretation?
2. Speaking in tongues is a language for whom?
3. When is it appropriate to use tongues in a church service?
4. According to the author may a person speak in tongues and then interpret their own tongue?

Chapter 11   Now that I know . . . what do I do?

Paul told the Corinthians that he wanted them to be educated in the gifts of the Spirit. We might be considering the very same question. How do I get more of the Spirit, and how do I best represent Him as I minister to others? How can I get a stronger flow of the Spirit in me? Do I really have to memorize how the gifts work?

The purpose of this study was to show how the gifts of the Holy Spirit work and then to use when ministering to others. In the West we must push through logic and reason to begin to move more comfortably in the gifts of God.[88] If we want to see God move more in His Spirit, then we have to give Him opportunity. Look around you most people have needs, some are lonely, depressed and there are even those who are arrogant and feel that God is just a crutch.

Where do I begin?

I usually have a huddle with God.[89] I pray, "God give me the eyes, ears and heart of Jesus." This helps me to be more aware of people around me.

---

[88] It is very difficult for us to accept things we cannot understand. It is easier to discount the supernatural activity of God.

[89] Spend time with God while praying in tongues. Quite often I will get a vision or word so that I know who God wants to minister to.

We have a winter visitor who gives me a number of $100 bills. He always says, "Rick, give these out to people who need the money." Pray and ask God who to give them to. One time he asked me to deliver $100 to someone who most needed it. I took the money and said to God, "Show me where to go to find the person who needs the money." I had a vision of a Safeway about 5 miles from our church.[90] I then drove to the Safeway Grocery. All the while I prayed, "God, let me see the person who is to get the money." I walked into Safeway and I walked over to the checkout area and my attention was drawn to a father and young son. There were just a few things in the basket, milk, bread and hamburger. I look at the little boy and then the man and said, "The Lord told me you needed this." I handed him the money and started to walk away. He yelled, "Pastor, I am out of work and this is all we could afford for my son and I."[91] He said, "Pastor, come back and talk with me. What kind of church goes around handing out money?" I walked back and talked with him for a few moments, and then said, "How may I pray for you?" As you read through this short story try to pick out the gifts of the Spirit that were manifested. When beginning in operating in the gifts of the Spirit stay in a small group of people. Learn by ministering to one another.

---

[90] I had a vision of this Safeway Grocery Store in response to my prayer, "Give me the eye . . . of Jesus."
[91] He was a single parent.

Non-church attending appreciate being prayed for

Outside of the church setting people are very open to be prayed for. Many share details of their lives that they have kept close to their heart. You are safe for them. It is even more exciting when you pray and they are healed.

At one point in my life, I was an avid golfer. Every Friday another pastor friend and I would play a round of golf together. Many times we would end up with a pair of other golfers (foursome). It was quite usual that the other two men would have very "vivid" language. Usually when the stories and language got pretty gross either my friend or I would pull the other two golfers aside and say, "You might want to be careful with your language and stories – that other guy is a pastor." On one occasion there was one guy that topped the charts in bad language. So my pastor friend pulled the same stunt that I had the week before. On this one occasion the colorful golfer stopped and said, "Tomorrow I will have surgery for a quadruple bypass, would you pray for me?"

Jesus healed me!

Several weeks later I was lining up on the 8th green "t" box and I heard someone yelling my name. I stopped and turned and our new friend with the quadruple bypass was running across the fairways towards me. When I saw him running, I thought "that was a fast recovery!" He ran up to me and gave me a big hug and then shouted, "Jesus healed me!"

When quarried further I found out that he had been healed on the spot when we prayed for him. When he went in for surgery the next day, the doctors could find nothing wrong with his heart. That healing would have never happened if we had not been willing to be open to the Holy Spirit.

God wants to move through you to touch the lives of others. Are you ready to ask Him to bring people to you who need His help?

Each gift of the spirit was presented separately to help understand how to identify what the Holy Spirit is doing while people are being ministered to. While I think that knowing the gifts are very important it is not important to target any one gift as you minister to others. Instead, allow yourself to be open to the Holy Spirit wants to do.

Group work:

1. Identify the dominant gifts of the Holy Spirit that God uses in you.

2. Do you know which gifts of the Spirit that God uses you frequently?

3. Why did the author describe each gift individually?

4. Make plans with this group to go treasure hunting in a large mall or large store like Wal-Mart.

Ministry functions of Jesus – Next book

¹ Now concerning spiritual gifts, brethren, I would not have you   ignorant.
⁴ Now there are diversities of gifts, but the same Spirit. ⁵ And there are differences of administrations, but the same Lord. ⁶ And there are diversities of operations, but it is the same God which worketh all in all. ⁷ But the manifestation of the Spirit is given to every man to profit withal. (1Corinthians 12:4-7)

We have just finished a study of the gifts of the Holy Spirit, as a follow up course we will look at the functions that Jesus makes available to us as Christians.[92]

I believe that when Paul said, "Now concerning spirituals or spiritual matters, I want you to know as much as you can about them. Learn how to apply them in your daily lives." Paul breaks the spirituals down into three sections. The first grouping is the gifts of the Spirit. The second is the ministry gifts or gifts assigned by Jesus. The third is amount of grace that you need to accomplish your task. This is from the Father. Part two, then will be about the ministry functions. We will discover what they are and then learn to walk in them.

---

[92] *⁵ And there are differences of administrations, but the same Lord. (1Corinthians 12.5)*

Suggested Essay

Final examination essay Name each of the gifts of the Spirit and define each one. Give some examples how these gifts might work, either from your own life or from the author's stories.

Suggested questions:

1. Name the nine gifts of the Spirit.

2. What is the goal of this course?

3. Does the author think that the gifts of the spirit are still in operation?

4. What are the three basic gifts of the Spirit? In the first three chapters of the Book of Revelation List the things that the Holy Spirit reveals about things past and present.

5. Act 9. 10-16 if the revelation of future facts and events is the gift of the word of Wisdom, the revelation of present and past facts and events is the gift of the word of Knowledge, identify those gifts in these passages.

6. Study the book of Jonah to find the gift of the Word of Knowledge and the gift of the Word of Wisdom.

7. List other examples of both gifts from the book of Jonah

8. What other examples can you find of these gifts in the Old Testament?

ACTS 27.10FF (PAUL IS DELIVERED FROM A STORM)

9. How might God do this for you?

10. What does this study tell you about God and the Church?

11. Pick out examples of the gift of the Word of Knowledge?

12. Pick out examples of the gift of the word of wisdom.

13. Have you been trying to use some of them in ministry? Does your church?

Matthew 8:23-27

14. How do we see the gift of faith active in Jesus?

15. Jesus experienced and lived all of the gifts, but what was he really saying to his disciples when he said that they had "little faith?" I think that it was another way for Jesus to say, "Don't you get it?"

16. What kind of reassurance does this give you?

17. The gift of faith can be for a short time to complete a single task, or it can be for a life-time, how have you experienced it?

Feeding the five thousand John 6.5-14

18. What gifts do you see in operation?

19. What process did Jesus use to build faith in his disciples"?

20. How did Jesus show that something special was about to happen?

21. How did people respond after the miracle?

22. List three examples from the Old and New Testament where the working of miracles can be identified.

Mark 9.14-1924.

23. Did the Spirit of God move perfectly in Jesus? How so?

25. Was Jesus truly in tune with the Word, the Father and the Spirit?

26. Is it possible for us to have that same sensitivity?

27. What exactly did Jesus mean when he said: *"Anything is possible if a   person believes?"*

[15] *"If (since) you love me, obey my commandments. 93* [16] *And I will ask the Father, and he will give you another Counsellor, who will never leave you.*

28. What can we ask of the Father when praying for people?

29. What does it mean to do the same works as Jesus? How many can you find in the book of Luke?

30. What does love of God have to do with the way people understand God?

31. Why is it important for Paul to say, *"I speak in tongues more than all of you?*

32. List out the benefits of tongues

33. Why do you think speaking in tongues is given such prominence in the Great commission?

34. What gifts of the Spirit does this gift open the doorway to?

35. Why are tongues a sign for the unbeliever outside the church service but not within the church service?

36. How does the author use tongues and interpretation?

38. Speaking in tongues is a language for whom?

39. When is it appropriate to use tongues in a church service?

40. According to the author may a person speak in tongues and then interpret their own tongue?

Suggested Reading

The gift of prophecy in the New Testament and today, by Wayne Grudem, 2000,Crossway Books, Crescent Street, Wheaton, Illinois 60187, ISBN 13:978-158134-243-7

Recommended internet Reading

Harald Bredesen

https://www.cbn.org/spirituallife/BibleStudyAndTheology/theholyspirit/Ross_Bredesen_One_of_a_Kind.aspx

Harald Bredesen

http://en.wikipedia.org/wiki/Harald_Bredesen

Gifts of the Holy Spirit

en.wikipedia.org/wiki/

Pastor Jim Feeny - A Pentecostal View of the gifts of the Spirit

http://www.jimfeeney.org/giftsofholyspirit.html

A guide to love, prayer and Mediation – description of the working of the Holy Spirit

http://www.thevoiceforlove.com/holy-spirit.html

Gifts of the Spirit – a perfect example of how an author removes the supernatural side of the gifts.

http://www.biblewriter.com/transformed7.htm

Bibliography

Dreams, Visions, and Spiritual Messages, Audrey Langdon, J.&J Publishers- Falls Church, Virginia

Satan is Alive and Well on Planet Earth, Zondervan, Hal Lindsey

The Fourth Dimension - Volume Two, Paul Yonggi Cho, Bridge Publishing

The Complete Biblical Library, R.R. Donnelly and Sons, Chicago Illinois 60606 *Springfield, Missouri-* ISBN 88-62537

Power Evangelism, John Wimber and Kevin Springer – Harper San Francisco and Gospel Light **ISBN:** 0830747966

The Gift of Prophecy in New Testament times and Today- Dr. Wayne Grudem Crossway Books- 2000-ISBN 978-58134-243-713:

*Yes, Lord –*Harald Bredesen and Pat King, Gospel Light, 2008, ISBN: 0830745351

Prophecy in Early Christianity and the Ancient Mediterranean World, David E. Aune, p. 3-Wlliam B Eerdmans Publishing Company- ISBN 0-8028-0635-X

– God's Empowering Presence, The Holy Spirit in the Letters of Paul – Gordon D. Fee -Hendrickson, publisher, 1994 –ISBN: 094357594X

They Speak with Other Tongues, John L Sherrill, Chosen Publishing
Company, 1991-ISBN: ISBN: 0800791304

.

5370525R00066

Made in the USA
San Bernardino, CA
03 November 2013